AUSTRALIA

Countering Violent Extremism in Australia and Abroad

A Framework for Characterising CVE Programs in Australia, the United States, and Europe

Andrew Lauland, Jennifer D. P. Moroney, John G. Rivers, Jacopo Bellasio, Kate Cameron

For more information on this publication, visit www.rand.org/t/RR2168

Library of Congress Cataloging-in-Publication Data is available for this publication.
ISBN: 978-1-9774-0243-1

Published by the RAND Corporation, Santa Monica, California and Canberra, Australia
© Copyright 2019 RAND Corporation
RAND® is a registered trademark.

Cover: Simon McGill

Support RAND
Make a tax-deductible charitable contribution at
www.rand.org/giving/contribute

www.rand.org

Preface

While the worldwide focus on countering violent extremism (CVE) is growing, it is not clear that the increase in programs that concentrate on CVE has been accompanied by a clear understanding of what approaches are most effective or, more broadly, what programs actually perform services of this type.

Significant differences appear in national-level strategy and approaches, how long government-funded efforts have been underway, and how governments and other partners and stakeholders work together. This project begins an attempt to close these gaps by identifying a general framework for understanding CVE programs, focusing in-depth on two promising CVE programs in Australia, and identifying programs with similar characteristics in the United States and Europe. The research in this report represents a starting point for further work, suggesting several potentially promising data sources either already available or in development that, if leveraged, could greatly enhance understanding of the nature of CVE efforts worldwide and which practices may be most effective in which contexts. Insights in this report will interest Australian, American, and European policymakers, practitioners, program managers, and academics who are working on CVE, as well as those interested in evaluating the effects of these types of efforts.

RAND is a research organization that develops solutions to public policy challenges to help make communities throughout the world safer and more secure, healthier and more prosperous. RAND is nonprofit, nonpartisan, and committed to the public interest.

RAND Ventures is a vehicle for investing in policy solutions. Philanthropic contributions support our ability to take the long view, tackle tough and often-controversial topics, and share our findings in innovative and compelling ways. Funding for this venture was provided by gifts from RAND supporters and income from operations.

This work was conducted by RAND Australia, working with the RAND Center for Asia Pacific Policy. RAND Australia is RAND's Canberra-based subsidiary that analyses defence, security, economic, and social issues for Australian clients. With a commitment to core values of quality and objectivity, RAND Australia combines local research talent with world-class experts from across RAND's global presence to solve complex Australian public policy problems.

For more information on RAND Australia or to contact our director, please visit www.rand.org/australia.

For more information on the RAND Center for Asia Pacific Policy, see www.rand.org/international_programs/capp.

RAND's research findings and recommendations do not necessarily reflect the policy preferences or interests of its clients, donors, or supporters.

Contents

Figures and Tables

Figures

Tables

Summary

One of the primary concerns of government and law enforcement in Australia, as well as of many other governments worldwide, is the threat of homegrown violent extremism. As a result, programs have proliferated in many nations more rapidly than has the understanding of these programs. In fact, relatively little is known about the basic types of and characteristics of the various countering violent extremism (CVE) programs and interventions that have been created around the world. Australia, Europe, and the United States have all made considerable investments in policies, programs, and interventions aimed at tackling violent radicalisation and extremism, but this increase in CVE program funding has not been accompanied by a growth in understanding of programs designed to prevent and tackle violent extremism and radicalisation.[1]

It is likely that much can be learned across programs and across continents. This report lays a foundation for future research by examining two promising CVE programs in Australia, identifying their primary distinguishing characteristics, and taking advantage of new and previously collected information on CVE programs in Europe and the United States to identify programs with similar characteristics and goals.

The objective of this study was to help program directors and policymakers in Australia place their programs in context and identify promising approaches internationally. The two example Australia pro-

---

[1]   See work by Harris-Hogan, Barrelle, and Zammit (2015).

grams could also serve as laboratories on how to achieve similar goals in other settings and provide partners a way to exchange information.

This limited-scope study focused on two ongoing CVE programs in Australia identified by the Australian Attorney-General's Department as being of high interest: (1) Multicultural New South Wales' *The Point*, an online magazine and resource for Australian youth, and (2) the Australian Multicultural Foundation's Community Awareness Training Manual—Building Resilience in the Community program (CAT), a train-the-trainer focused program to provide key stakeholders with the tools to detect and counter radicalisation. The project team developed a general framework for characterising CVE programs and then collected information on and interviewed staff at the two Australian programs. Using this framework and the results of the program interviews and data collection, we characterised the two Australian programs according to their primary characteristics, and then we examined existing and publicly available information on CVE programs in Europe and the United States to identify programs with similar goals, approaches, and target populations. Although this study was neither a rigorous assessment of the extent to which certain models or types of programs exist in Australia, Europe, and the United States nor an evaluation of the individual programs and their effectiveness, we nonetheless identified six European and U.S. programs with similar goals and activity types to the Australian programs. This method for mapping programs against goals and activity types could facilitate information exchange across programs in the future.

Our review identified three European programs with characteristics similar to *The Point*, two European programs with characteristics similar to CAT, and one U.S. program with characteristics similar to CAT. Three of the six programs we identified had available evaluation material that might be useful to program staff in Australia; although we did not identify such material in the other three programs during the course of the study, those programs might have relevant material that we simply did not identify.

In the course of identifying a set of programs with similar goals and activities that may benefit from sharing information between their respective staffs and those of *The Point* and CAT, some interesting characteristics did begin to emerge. First, each program identified as a counterpart to *The Point* appeared to have a strong online presence and associated communities. Areas where these programs differed from *The Point*, and that may interest *The Point* staff, were engagement methods for their target groups—ranging from an award competition to empowerment efforts—and the use of wider varieties of media, including cartoons, online video, and other formats. Second, the European programs seemed to have more-direct approaches to developing alternative narratives than *The Point*. Whereas *The Point* seemed to take a more subtle approach of providing a safe space for conversation, allowing government-funded expression of support for opinions of all types, including those counter to the government (as long as not violent), the European programs identified by the study more directly engaged in developing alternative narratives: either asking young people themselves to do so or providing target groups with information to defuse extremist rhetoric. Whether either approach is superior, and in what context, are important questions for future research that were beyond the scope of this study.

The three programs similar to CAT seemed to share a common trait in that they provided fairly broad bases of services. This is not necessarily dissimilar from CAT, because interviews with CAT staff suggested that the program provided a host of other services when needed, which may have changed over the years of program operation based on demand. However, the services offered by the European and U.S. programs may have been more explicit and ongoing distinct program components than in CAT. More notably, this suggests that programs of this nature may commonly offer a suite of services and activities to participants, rather than providing only a single service. Whether this approach is effective, and what the ideal mix of services might be and in what context, are important questions for future research that were beyond the scope of this study.

The report concludes by identifying a range of future lines of inquiry and research questions that were suggested by this study. This research was conducted in 2016.

Acknowledgments

The authors wish to thank the staff of Multicultural New South Wales and the Australian Multicultural Foundation for generously providing their time to participate in interviews to answer follow-up questions over the course of the project, and for sharing their invaluable insights into countering violent extremism, increasing social cohesion, and related efforts. The authors also wish to thank the staff of the Australian Attorney-General's Department for their guidance and support throughout the study. We are grateful for the insightful quality assurance reviews of this report provided by Todd Helmus from RAND and Professor Michele Grossman from Deakin University. In addition, the authors wish to thank Anita Chandra, Henry Willis, Hans Pung, and Erin Smith for their guidance and assistance throughout the project. We are grateful to the contributions of Roslyn Richardson for her background research that contributed to this report. Lastly, the authors wish to thank Rafiq Dossani, Scott W. Harold, and the RAND Center for Asia Pacific Policy for generously supporting this project and making it possible.

Abbreviations

ADFYWIAD	Advisory Directorate for Youth, Women and Imams' Active Development
AFP	Australian Federal Police
AGD	Australian Attorney-General's Department
AMF	Australian Multicultural Foundation
C7	Cypher 7 A.D.
CAT	Community Awareness Training Manual—Building Resilience in the Community program
CVE	countering violent extremism
DHS	U.S. Department of Homeland Security
EU	European Union
HA	Australian Department of Home Affairs
HVE	homegrown violent extremism
IACP	Internal Association of Chiefs of Police
LST	Living Safe Together
MCM	Montgomery County Model
MCW	Muslim Council of Wales
NSW	New South Wales
OCP	DHS Office of Community Partnerships
OCR	DHS Office of Congressional Relations

P/CVE	preventing and countering of violent extremism
P2P	Peer 2 Peer: Challenging Extremism
WAG	Welsh Assembly Government
WORDE	World Organization for Resource Development and Education

CHAPTER ONE

Introduction

Homegrown Violent Extremism in Australia

One of the primary concerns of law enforcement in Australia is the threat of homegrown violent extremism (HVE). Australia is, per capita, one of the largest source countries of foreign fighters to Syria and Iraq, with more than 200 Australians having travelled to participate in conflicts in those countries. However, as of 2016, authorities also estimate that approximately 40 individuals have returned to Australia from conflict zones (this figure does not include children and other family members) (Brandis, 2016a). The influence that these returnees and conflicts abroad may have on Australia and its communities is potentially profound.

HVE can encompass a wide range of ideologies and manifestations, but its central defining characteristic is a threat to a nation that comes from within. As defined by the International Association of Chiefs of Police (IACP), a homegrown violent extremist is

> a citizen or long-term resident in a western country who has rejected western cultural values, beliefs, and norms in favor of a violent extremist ideology. The homegrown violent extremist intends to commit terrorism inside western countries or against their interests. (International Association of Chiefs of Police, Committee on Terrorism, Countering Violent Extremism Working Group, p. 5)

IACP also suggests that HVE can encompass a wide range of activities, including "those who encourage, endorse, condone, justify, or support the commission of a violent criminal act" and motivations across a broad spectrum that includes "political, ideological, religious, social, or economic goals" (quoted in U.S. Department of Justice, Office of Community Oriented Policing Services, 2014).

From 2014, when the Australian terrorism threat level was raised to "probable," to the end of 2016, 57 people were charged in 27 counter-terrorism operations in Australia (Helsel, 2016). As of September 2016, approximately 200 people were being investigated for a range of behaviours, including providing support to individuals and groups in conflict zones through funding and facilitation (Brandis, 2016b).

However, virtually no nation is immune to the threats of radicalisation and homegrown violent extremism, with attacks by naturalised citizens occurring over the past several years in Australia, the United States, and throughout Europe. Since 2006, these types of attacks have accounted for nearly 70 percent of terrorism-related deaths in the West (Institute for Economics and Peace, 2015). As a result, efforts to cope with violent extremism have grown rapidly across the globe. Such efforts are commonly labelled *countering violent extremism (CVE)*. Although the term *CVE* was not used widely in the United States until 2015, it has been used in Australia since 2010. No single consensus definition of the term exists, but *CVE* has been defined by one author as

> the use of non-coercive means to dissuade individuals or groups from mobilising towards violence and to mitigate recruitment, support, facilitation or engagement in ideologically motivated terrorism by non-state actors in furtherance of political objectives. (Khan, 2015)

Others have observed that "CVE has gone from a rhetorical commitment to an increasingly prominent subfield of counterterrorism policy and practice" while noting the importance of—but lack of agreement on—a definition of CVE (Romaniuk, 2015).

What is clearer is what CVE is not. CVE is distinct from classical counterterrorism efforts, which in the modern era depend more on the use of law enforcement (acting in its capacity as enforcer of the peace), the military, technology, and intelligence. CVE has some characteristics in common with community policing efforts but is, again, distinct in its focus on preventing radicalisation to violence based on ideological beliefs, rather than crime alone. Many CVE programs and frameworks have focused on the social-cohesion and community-resilience dimensions of soft-power approaches to mitigating violent extremism, as distinct from the more securitised lens of counterterrorism proper.

During a September 24, 2014, United Nations Security Council meeting chaired by U.S. President Barack Obama, the council adopted Resolution 2178 to create a new policy and legal framework for international action in response to the foreign terrorist fighter threat worldwide. For the first time, the council underscored that CVE was an essential element of an effective response to the threat posed by foreign terrorist fighters (U.S. Department of Justice, undated). Specifically, Resolution 2178 recognised that

> addressing the threat posed by foreign terrorist fighters requires comprehensively addressing underlying factors, including by preventing radicalisation to terrorism, stemming recruitment, inhibiting foreign terrorist fighter travel, disrupting financial support to foreign terrorist fighters, countering violent extremism, which can be conducive to terrorism, countering incitement to terrorist acts motivated by extremism or intolerance, promoting political and religious tolerance, economic development and social cohesion and inclusiveness, ending and resolving armed conflicts, and facilitating reintegration and rehabilitation. (United Nations Security Council, 2014)

Study Objectives

Although the worldwide focus on CVE is growing, it is not clear that the increase in programs focused on CVE has been accompanied by a clear understanding of what approaches are being taken, let alone which are most effective. Significant differences appear across nations in strategy and approaches, how long organised efforts have been underway, and how government and other partners and stakeholders work together.

Programs have proliferated in many nations more rapidly than has understanding of them. As a result, little is known even about the basic types of and characteristics of the various CVE programs and interventions that are underway. This proliferation has occurred in Europe, where, over the past decade, considerable investments have been made by the European Union (EU) and its member states in policies, programs, and interventions aimed at tackling violent radicalisation and extremism, both within and outside of the EU's borders. This increase in CVE program funding, however, has not been accompanied by a growth in evidence-based understanding of the landscape of programs aimed at preventing and tackling violent extremism and radicalisation. In the United States in 2016, the U.S. Department of Homeland Security (DHS) announced its first round of funding to support CVE programs: $10 million[1] in competitive awards for CVE programs through the DHS Office of Community Partnerships (OCP; DHS, undated-b). Australia has been an early leader in CVE, investing in the Building Resilient Communities stream funding and establishment of the CVE Centre in 2010, followed by a $64 million investment in CVE programs in 2014 (Abbott and Brandis, 2014).

It is likely that much is to be learned across programs and across continents. The purpose of the study described in this report was to provide a foundation for future research by examining two promising CVE programs in Australia, identifying their primary distinguishing characteristics, and leveraging new and previously collected information on CVE programs in Europe and the United States to identify programs with similar characteristics and goals. The objective of this study was to help program directors and policymakers in Australia place their programs in context and identify promising approaches internationally. The two example Australia programs could also serve

---

[1] All monetary values throughout this report relating to expenditures are in the funding entity's home currency; for example, expenditures by U.S. entities are in U.S. dollars, and expenditures by Australian entities are in Australian dollars.

as laboratories on how to achieve similar goals in other settings and serve as partners to exchange information.

This limited-scope study, which ended in 2016, focused on two ongoing CVE programs in Australia identified by the Australian Attorney-General's Department (AGD) as promising and of high interest.[2] The project team developed a general framework for characterising CVE programs and then collected information on and interviewed staff at the two Australian programs. Using this framework and the results of the program interviews and data collection, we characterised the two Australian programs according to their primary characteristics, and then we examined existing and publicly available information on CVE programs in Europe and the United States to identify programs with similar goals, approaches, and target populations. Although this study was neither a rigorous assessment of the extent to which certain models or types of programs exist in Australia, Europe, and the United States, nor an evaluation of the individual programs and their effectiveness, we identified six European and U.S. programs with goals and activity types similar to the Australian programs. This method for mapping programs against goals and activity types could facilitate information exchange across continents. Our research was quite limited in scope due to tight resource constraints, so we played to our strengths by using data from the United States and the EU rather than, for example, Canada, Southeast Asia, or elsewhere.

How This Report Is Organised

Chapter Two provides a brief overview of the methodology used in the study. Chapter Three provides a brief overview of the landscape of CVE efforts in Australia to provide context for the two Australian CVE programs profiled in the report. Chapters Four and Five provide descriptive overviews of the two Australian CVE programs and their

---

[2]   From RAND's perspective, we wanted to look at two promising programs that had been ongoing for a number of years with different applications and in different states or territories. A full description of the criteria is included in this report.

primary characteristics. Chapter Six introduces a simple framework for characterising the Australian CVE programs and discusses our efforts and findings from a review of U.S. and European CVE programs. Chapter Seven concludes with a summary of our findings and some observations regarding future research in Australia and worldwide in this important and dynamic field.

Methodology

Australian CVE Programs

Australia was selected as the country of focus for this project because of that nation's early focus on and investment in CVE, its prior experience with the threat of HVE, and the willingness of the Australian government to identify programs of interest for further study.

To combat the threat of HVE, Australia has adopted a comprehensive strategy that is based on a whole-of-government approach involving five core elements: challenging violent extremist ideologies, stopping people from becoming terrorists, shaping the global environment, disrupting terrorist activity within Australia, and providing effective response and recovery (Council of Australian Governments, 2015). As part of this strategy, Australia has increasingly invested in a wide variety of CVE programs.

Advancing the 2010 Building Resilient Communities and CVE Centre investments, in 2014 the Australian government announced that it would invest more than $64 million in measures to help combat homegrown terrorism and deter Australians from joining overseas terrorist activities (Abbott and Brandis, 2014). The measures Prime Minister Tony Abbott announced included $13.4 million to strengthen community engagement programs in Australia, with an emphasis on preventing young Australians from becoming involved with extremist groups. In 2015, this $13.4 million included $1.6 million for the Living Safe Together (LST) grants program (Abbott and Brandis, 2014), with an additional $365,122 added to the LST program later the same year (Australian National Audit Office, 2016). In 2015, $21.7 million was

7

also provided over four years for the Combating Terrorist Propaganda program to fund social media monitoring and analysis capabilities. The intent of this program was to reduce extremist material online, develop a portal through which members of the public could report extremist material, and provide assistance to community groups working with vulnerable individuals (Abbott and Brandis, 2014).

In 2016, the government, under Prime Minister Malcolm Turnbull, announced that it was investing a further $5 million to support communities affected by violent extremism and to prevent young people from falling for the allure of violent extremists online (Brandis, and Keenan, 2016). The government package included the following amounts:

- $4 million to enable the New South Wales (NSW) helpline to be rolled out across the country to help families and other frontline workers, such as teachers and community leaders, seek help for young people at risk of online grooming by terrorists
- $1 million for the e-Safety Commissioner to strengthen Australia's prevention strategies and reach young people before they become vulnerable to terrorism.

In discussions with us, AGD identified two ongoing programs as being of high interest: Multicultural NSW's *The Point Magazine* (*The Point Magazine*, 2018) and the Australian Multicultural Foundation's (AMF's) Community Awareness Training Manual—Building Resilience in the Community program (CAT; AMF, undated).

We developed an interview guide to collect information on the two programs using a questionnaire developed as part of IMPACT Europe,[1] an EU-funded project that conducted in 2014 a survey of CVE programs throughout Europe as a model (IMPACT Europe,

---

[1] IMPACT Europe stands for Innovative Methods and Procedures to Assess Counter-Violent-Radicalisation Techniques in Europe. This project was funded by the European Union through its Seventh Framework Program with the aim to fill the gap in knowledge and understanding of what works in preventing and tackling violent radicalisation and extremism, and to help front-line workers, policymakers and other parties operating in the field of counter-violent-radicalisation. For further details, see www.impacteurope.eu.

2015). Interviews were conducted in August and September 2016 with staff at the two programs and were supplemented with open-source material and material provided by the two programs, including annual reports and program evaluations.

No single, universally accepted framework exists for characterising CVE programs. Accordingly, we adopted a framework based on the searchable characteristics of CVE programs in the IMPACT Europe database. As of late 2017, only the IMPACT database is searchable at the level of attributes desired for this study. As shown in Table 2.1, among other frameworks for analysis, the IMPACT Europe CVE database characterises CVE programs by six key attributes:

- group of focus
- unit of focus
- whether the program is focused on a particular ideology
- the goal of the program's interventions
- the primary type of activity engaged in by the program
- the program's effectiveness level.

Study team members coded each Australian CVE program selected for the study by making judgements along each of the first five attributes to develop general "type" profiles for the programs to assist in identifying similar programs in the United States and Europe. We also examined any evidence of effectiveness associated with each program and the processes used for evaluation. Our findings regarding the two Australian programs are summarised in Chapters Four and Five. To make the information more accessible, the chapters are structured to provide a brief overview of the program, followed by more-detailed sections on

- goals and overall approach
- focus (group of focus, unit of focus, and ideology)
- activity type
- evidence of effectiveness.

Table 2.1
IMPACT Europe Searchable CVE Program Characteristics and Types

Group of Focus	Unit of Focus	Ideology	Intervention Goal	Activity Type	Effectiveness Level
Individuals vulnerable to radicalisation	Individual	Religious	Disengage	Educational and mentoring	Strong
Radicalised individuals	Group	Political	Suppress	Informational	Medium
Offenders	Network	Other	Prevent	Sanctioning	Weak
Prisoners	Multiple		Mitigate	Social and positive alternatives	Nonsignificant
Financers				Therapeutic	
Friends and family				Enabling organisations	
Communities					
Policymakers and journalists					
Social and healthcare workers					
Education sector and religious leaders					
Criminal justice					
Other					

Identification of Comparable Programs

To identify potentially similar programs, we turned to prior research and open-source material, including academic literature, government documents, news reports, and websites, with a focus on Europe and the United States. To identify a set of comparable programs, we attempted to match the coded key attributes of the two Australian programs to programs characterised by those same attributes in the United States and Europe. However, because limited information is available about

CVE programs, and because this information is often incomplete or collected in different formats, we searched for matches on what we considered to be the two most important attributes: program goal and activity type. We also focused on program goal and activity type as the primary characteristics of interest because many programs focused on multiple groups, units, and ideologies simultaneously. For example, many programs serve both individuals vulnerable to radicalisation and their family members, or seek to address both political and religious ideologies. It is also likely that tactics that are effective for programs focused on one ideology may be transferable to programs focusing on other ideologies.

Because this method returned a large number of programs that were somewhat similar to the two Australian programs, we also reviewed additional open-source information to select those programs with the greatest similarity to the two selected Australian programs. The data sources reviewed to identify comparable programs in Europe and the United States are discussed briefly below and in greater detail in Chapter Six.

Europe

Preventing and countering violent extremism (P/CVE) is consistently at the top of the EU agenda, particularly in the Middle East and North Africa (European Commission, 2017). Across the EU, member states have adopted increasingly complex and nuanced counter-radicalisation strategies composed of programs with different goals and implemented by different actors and groups. The EU approach to preventing and countering violent extremism and radicalisation and has been characterised by a broad focus on different types of ideological motivation. Existing programs and initiatives look not only at extremism of an Islamist or jihadist nature but also at right-wing, left-wing, ethnonationalist, separatist, animal rights, and other forms of single-issue extremism (Vidino and Brandon, 2012).

The EU focus on and commitment to preventing radicalisation and violent extremism was most recently renewed in the 2015 *European Agenda on Security*, in which this issue was identified as one of the Union's three core security priorities for the 2015–2020 period

(European Commission, 2015). It is not surprising, therefore, that a number of programs and initiatives comparable to the Australian ones discussed above could be identified through a review of recent publications focusing on programs countering and preventing violent extremism in Europe.

The need to identify good and promising practices related to CVE has been expressed in a number of key documents adopted by EU bodies in recent years. Various initiatives are funded by EU institutions to advance the understanding of what approaches are most effective in CVE. One of these, the Radicalisation Awareness Network, is an umbrella network that connects people involved in preventing and tackling radicalisation and violent extremism throughout Europe. The Radicalisation Awareness Network provides its members with working groups and other platforms to meet and exchange ideas, knowledge, and experiences related to CVE. Practices identified as promising or effective are collected and presented to practitioners through publications, conferences, and capacity-building events.

Another EU-funded initiative focusing on identifying promising CVE practice is the previously discussed IMPACT Europe project. This project developed an online evaluation toolkit to enable P/CVE practitioners and stakeholders to conduct a robust evaluation of policies and interventions preventing and tackling violent radicalisation and extremism. The toolkit also helps professionals in the public and voluntary sectors to integrate promising practices into the design and implementation of future programs.[2]

We reviewed information on CVE programs in Europe available from these two sources to identify CVE programs in Europe with similar characteristics to the two Australian programs, finding several of note.

United States

While a coordinated approach to CVE at the federal level in the United States is less mature than it is in the EU or in Australia, many advances have been made since 2011. In August 2011, the U.S. govern-

---

[2]   Abbott and Brandis, 2014. For further details please visit www.impacteurope.eu.

ment issued its first formal, national-level CVE strategy titled *Empowering Local Partners to Prevent Violent Extremism in the United States* (DHS, 2011a). This strategy was followed closely with the release of the *Strategic Implementation Plan for Empowering Local Partners to Prevent Violent Extremism in the United States* (DHS, 2011b) later that year. In February 2015, the White House held a three-day CVE summit to discuss steps that the United States and its partners could take to develop community-oriented CVE approaches. Later that year, DHS established OCP to act as the lead federal coordinator for U.S. CVE efforts.

DHS's 2011 CVE strategic implementation plan was updated in 2016 to respond to "the current dynamics of violent extremism and reflect experience and knowledge acquired over the last five years" (DHS, 2016, p. 1). This revised plan reaffirms the notion that an effective CVE strategy must consist of coordinated efforts at the national, local, and individual levels and must focus on integrating CVE concepts into existing programs through collaboration. In January 2017, $10 million in grants were awarded to fund or partially fund 31 programs across the nation (DHS, 2017). Appendix B provides an overview of these programs by location and type.

Despite these advances, as of late 2016 there is no centralised source of information about U.S. CVE programs similar to IMPACT Europe.[3] Therefore, to identify analogous U.S. programs, we reviewed publicly available material on each of the 31 programs that received a grant from DHS Office of Congressional Relations (OCR), once again using the key attributes of the two Australian programs as screening criteria.

This approach had two major limitations. First, because publicly available information about grant awardees included only the name of the organisation and general award category,[4] for 13 of the 31 awards it was not possible to determine the specific program within a

---

[3]   One of the nine objectives in the U.S. DHS CVE strategy is to build a database of U.S. CVE programs.

[4]   Grants were awarded for programs across five broad categories: Developing Resilience, Training and Engagement, Managing Interventions, Challenging the Narrative, and Building Capacity.

given organisation's portfolio that was to be funded through the OCR grant, reducing the number of potential programs for comparison to 18. Second, because many of the funded programs were either under development or were in their infancy when this research was conducted in 2016, despite the fact that we were able to identify a number of matches based on general program description, often not enough information was available to draw useful comparisons for the purposes of this study. Accordingly, we then searched open-source information on other U.S. CVE programs, including program websites, government and academic literature, and media reports. Through this method, we identified one other U.S. CVE program that was comparable to one of the Australian programs.

Analysis

Once comparable programs in Europe and the United States were identified, we gathered additional information about each program. Because study resources were limited, we drew only from publicly available information on the European and U.S. programs. Chapter Six includes brief vignettes summarising each program identified as similar and identifies key similarities and differences relative to the comparable Australian program. Where an evaluation had occurred and was available, we note it. In total, we identified six comparable programs across Europe and the United States, with three programs similar to *The Point* and three similar to CAT. Half of the programs had conducted some form of evaluation that was available to us. These results are discussed in greater detail in Chapters Six and Seven.

CHAPTER THREE

Countering Violent Extremism in Australia

The Australian government is highly focused on consolidating its national security functions to include CVE. As of December 2017, with the creation of a new Department of Home Affairs (HA), the CVE portfolio has recently moved to HA from AGD. The CVE Centre was established in 2010 as a result of a counterterrorism white paper that acknowledged the risk of homegrown terrorism and highlighted the importance of building a strong and resilient community to resist violent extremism and terrorism (McCelland, 2010; Australian Government, 2010).

The vision of the CVE Centre is to reduce the risk of homegrown terrorism by strengthening Australians' resilience to radicalisation and assisting individuals in disengaging from violent extremist influences and beliefs. The centre's approach previously consisted of four complimentary tiers of activities:

- **Building strength in diversity and social participation**, which focuses on the societal drivers that can lead to disengagement and isolation by funding multicultural community initiatives and other social policy programs to enhance community harmony, improve migrant integration, and strengthen economic participation
- **Targeted work with vulnerable communities and institutions**, which provides support for communities to help them identify and prevent people from moving down the path of radicalisation to violence and includes the development of community information resources and training packages

- **Addressing terrorist propaganda online**, which confronts online radicalisation and challenges terrorist propaganda with the goal of limiting its appeal, reducing access to extremist material online, and empowering community voices to combat extremist narratives
- **Diversion and deradicalisation**, which delivers early-intervention programs to help people move away from violent ideologies and reconnect with their communities.

The CVE Centre within HA coordinates and manages a number of domestic partnerships across multiple levels of government to carry out this strategy. These partnerships are shown in Figure 3.1 and are described below.

The role of the **social policy agencies** is to implement policies aimed at promoting social inclusion and preventing marginalisation. These policies can also address grievances, which may stem from bar-

Figure 3.1
Government Partners of Australia's CVE Centre

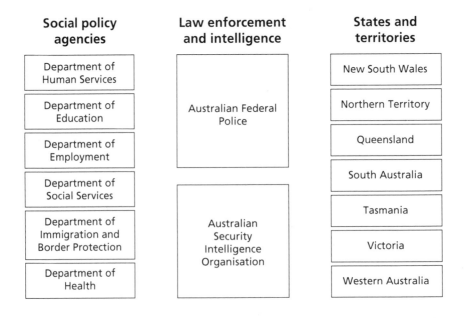

Social policy agencies	Law enforcement and intelligence	States and territories
Department of Human Services	Australian Federal Police	New South Wales
Department of Education		Northern Territory
Department of Employment		Queensland
Department of Social Services		South Australia
Department of Immigration and Border Protection	Australian Security Intelligence Organisation	Tasmania
		Victoria
Department of Health		Western Australia

riers to social and economic participation. Examples of social policies include

- education and training programs
- individual support services
- youth initiatives, including mentoring and job advice
- family, peer, and community support
- community outreach.

The focal point for **law enforcement and intelligence** is HA, whose portfolio now encompasses the Australian Federal Police (AFP), which is actively involved in CVE initiatives, including community engagement, building social cohesion, and increasing resilience within diverse communities. These activities help identify people who may be at risk of radicalisation and assist in diverting individuals away from this pathway. The AFP also contributes to whole-of-government initiatives aimed at empowering communities to challenge extremist messages and support communities in the non-violent expression of their views (Australian Government, 2018a). Also within the HA portfolio is the Australian Security Intelligence Organisation, which conducts a variety of activities to help identify individuals and groups intent on acting on extremist beliefs. These activities include engagement with influential community and religious figures and investigations relating to identified extremists or extremist threats (Australian Government, 2018a).

State and territory government agencies have also established policies and programs to foster cooperative relationships with local communities. In addition, the states and territories contribute to the Countering Violent Extremism Sub-Committee of the Australia–New Zealand Counter-Terrorism Committee, which is a vehicle for coordination and collaboration between the states and territories and at the federal level (Australian Government, 2018a).

In addition to collaboration and coordination within government, the CVE Centre also partners with local communities, which are best positioned to identify and directly influence the vulnerability of at-risk individuals. Partners include local councils, faith-based groups, sports clubs, and youth groups, a number of which are funded through the previously discussed LST grants program and Building Community Resilience/Youth Mentoring Program, which was a pilot.

The LST program was established in 2014 and ran from 2015 to 2016 to support community-based, nongovernmental organisations and local government organisations in developing new and innovative services for individuals at risk of violent extremism (Australian National Audit Office, 2016). In 2016, 28 programs were listed on the LST website, although we know that this number has changed and has likely been reduced. For example, the Building Community Resilience/Youth Mentoring Program was cancelled in 2012. Figure 3.2 provides an overview of these programs in 2016 according to the LST website by location and type.

The CVE Centre also engages with international partners and academia to foster collaboration and information sharing on best practice approaches and to leverage the most current knowledge and expertise. Academic research and an understanding of international best practices are seen as crucial to ensure an understanding of violent

Figure 3.2
Summary of CVE Programs

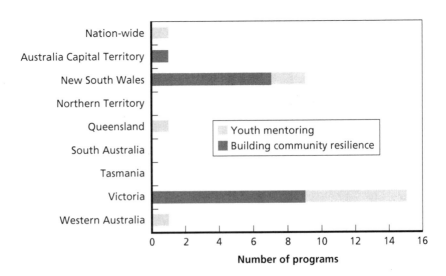

extremism, including the reasons for individuals becoming radicalised (Australian Government, 2018b).

We consulted with AGD (which at the time of research housed the CVE Centre) to identify promising CVE initiatives for inclusion in the study. Ultimately, AGD and the study team identified two programs for inclusion. The programs were selected because they have different foci and intervention approaches, providing some breadth. Both programs have also been up and running for several years, providing time for their respective approaches to mature and increasing the likelihood that data would be available to assess program effectiveness. Taking into account the aforementioned criteria along with AGD's recommendations, we identified the following two programs:

- *The Point Magazine*, an online publication administered by the New South Wales state government body Multicultural NSW
- the Community Awareness Training Manual—Building Resilience in the Community program (CAT), which is administered by the Australian Multicultural Foundation (AMF), an independent organisation that trains communities, service providers, and young people across Australia to recognise signs of radicalisation and develop strategies to assist affected individuals.

The next two chapters provide an overview of these two programs, drawing on interviews with knowledgeable program staff and review of open-source materials and documents provided by program staff.

CHAPTER FOUR

Multicultural New South Wales: *The Point Magazine*

Overview

The Point is an online magazine (or, as it describes itself on its website, an online resource) that targets younger readers and was first published in July 2013.[1] *The Point* publicly identifies its goal as being to engage and inform readers about news and current events with a specific focus on the effect that overseas conflicts have on local communities; it also provides content on local and international politics, religion, society, culture, and technology. *The Point* published 20 issues between 2013 and 2015, and ten issues in 2016.

Facts About *The Point*

Group of focus:
- Individuals vulnerable to radicalisation
- Friends and family

Communities:
- Policymakers and journalists
- Education sector and religious leaders

Unit of focus:
- Group

Ideology:
- Religious

Intervention goal:
- Prevent

Activity type:
- Educational and mentoring
- Informational

The online magazine is administered by Multicultural NSW, a state government body responsible for promoting and monitoring the multicultural principles set out in the Multicultural NSW Act 2000. Notably, *The Point* clearly acknowledges on its website that it is funded by the Australian federal government. *The Point* is funded through a

---

[1]   *The Point Magazine* can be accessed at http://www.thepointmagazine.com.au.

grant provided by the Countering Violent Extremism Sub-Committee of the Australia–New Zealand Counter-Terrorism Committee. According to interviews with program staff, funding totalled $73,000 over the 2012–2013 financial year, was $93,000 in the 2013–2014 financial year, and increased to $273,000 during the 2015–2016 financial year.[2]

Goals and Approach to CVE

In interviews, staff members from *The Point* indicated that they view violent extremism as fundamentally a social cohesion issue.[3] The staff also described violent extremism as fundamentally an issue that affects relations between communities in Australia. *The Point* has a specific focus on the effect that overseas conflicts have on local communities in Australia, and *The Point* staff noted multiple examples of the role that such conflicts and, more broadly, the global counterterrorist environment in general have had on community harmony. Interviewees noted that, as a result of conflicts abroad, local communities in Australia with ties to nations or groups involved in conflicts abroad have either been perceived as a threat by others or have faced internal threats to their communities. These tensions have played out in schoolyards, on the side of sporting fields, and between families, and these tensions have also manifested themselves in property damage and even acts of violence.

Recognising the direct influence that conflicts abroad, whether tribal, sectarian, or involving Australia and a foreign nation, can have at home, *The Point* identified one of its primary goals as building resil-

---

[2]   This funding covered the salary of *The Point Magazine*'s editor from 2013 to 2015. From July 2015 on, the funding was increased to cover the salaries of two staff: the editor and a principal writer. The project grant also covers the costs associated with the delivery of a small number of training projects and management of the website. Multicultural NSW is currently seeking alternative sources of funding for *The Point Magazine*. This includes pursuing sponsorship from private sector organisations and developing co-funding arrangements with other government agencies.

[3]   Unless otherwise noted, all interviews with *The Point* staff occurred on August 26, 2016, or September 1, 2016.

ience amongst local communities to deal with such conflicts. *The Point* leadership noted that, in addition to the result of actual acts of violent extremism and terrorism within Australia, the mere threat of these acts affects social cohesion in a way that must be managed as a component of combatting those who would do harm to the country and suggested that this effect is likely an explicit goal of extremists:

> Violent extremists themselves thrive on that tension. They're actually trying to incite division. And so beyond any particular act of violence. . . . their aim is to promote fear and hate and division within societies, and we need to counter more than just the violence involved in violence extremism. We need to counter the fear, the hate, and the division that they're seeking to perpetrate within our society as well.

However, program staff noted that the relationship between violent extremism and its subsequent detrimental effects on social cohesion is far clearer and more widely accepted than its opposite: the influence that improved social cohesion can have on countering violent extremism and its related impacts:

> Social cohesion can only have an indirect relationship to preventing an act of terrorist violence. Acts of terrorist violence and the very threat of violent extremists themselves has direct, identifiable, nameable, measurable impact on social cohesion and we need to do something about that.

Significantly, *The Point* staff indicated that, in their view, improvements in social cohesion were only a part of the system of programs and efforts needed to counter violent extremism, explicitly noting that their own efforts would not prevent someone from becoming a terrorist, stating flatly, "We don't make that claim." Despite this, staff stressed the importance and utility to the CVE enterprise of explicitly acknowledging the relationship between the two, noting that increasing social cohesion was often used as a "euphemism," in the staff's words, for CVE. Instead, a decline in social cohesion should be viewed as an important potential outcome of violent extremism. As is discussed below, *The Point* staff see their magazine's role as directly tackling the most contentious issues. If not dealt with constructively, extremists could manipulate these issues and could negatively affect social cohesion significantly even though they do not directly seek to exploit such issues.

While highlighting the concrete nature of the influences that terrorist acts and the threat of these acts can have on social cohesion, *The Point* staff suggested the CVE activities should be placed into the same framework that is typically used by emergency management:

> It's a reframing of the question, and that requires us to think beyond preventative counter terrorism and to actually talk about CVE within a full continuum. . . . We actually revert to the emergency management language, which says we need a response and recovery aspect of CVE.

In this view, the emergency management framework, which commonly consists of five phases (Prepare, Prevent, Respond, Recover, and Mitigate), would be applied not only to an act of violent extremism but also to the threat of violent extremism itself, as if it were an event. In this framework, *The Point*'s role would fall somewhere along the spectrum of helping communities in Australia to prepare for, prevent, respond to, recover from, and mitigate the results that the threat of violent extremism may have in Australia.

Focus (Group of Focus, Unit of Focus, and Ideology)

The Point primarily focuses on young audiences and, implicitly, members of communities that may be affected at home by overseas conflicts, spanning a variety of religious and ethnic groups. Based on interviews and a review of *The Point*'s published materials, it seems likely that *The Point* leadership would broadly define the magazine's target audience as "globally aware and politically active younger readers in multicultural Australia" (Harman, Bedford, and Fares, 2018), as well as "communities, researchers, aspiring journalists, and the established media" (Multicultural NSW, 2016).

During interviews, staff referred to events in Iraq, Syria, Mali, and Somalia. The November 2016 edition of *The Point* features prominent articles involving Pakistan and Kashmir (India). Earlier editions included articles related to Sudan, Turkey, and Iran.

In addition to targeting a diverse set of individuals with a range of religious and ethnic identities, while specifically targeting younger people, leadership of the *The Point* seek to reach out to and engage with several different groups and strata within multicultural communities. During interviews, *The Point* staff cited interactions with audiences ranging from community leaders (who might use information gleaned within their own communities or express their views through *The Point* as a forum) to groups, communities, and individuals, including those who might be, or already have been, the targets of radicalisation efforts.

The Point is available online and is circulated directly to an independent subscription base of 350 and to 4,100 contacts on Multicultural NSW's EmailLink database. From July 2013 to June 2016, *The Point* reached 56,293 readers and recorded 126,269 page views during 69,931 total sessions, with most readers accessing the website through organic search, direct search, or social media referrals (Multicultural NSW, 2016).

Through the effective use of online outreach strategies such as search engine optimisation, *The Point* staff has been able to increase the magazine's readership since its inception, as depicted in Figure 4.1.

Activity Type

The central activity of *The Point* is its online magazine. Both the editor and the main reporter at *The Point* have journalism backgrounds, and both have worked in community advocacy roles.

In interviews, staff described the magazine as an extension and evolution of earlier CVE-related work undertaken by Multicultural NSW based on lessons learned from that work. Representatives from Multicultural NSW noted that the organisation had previously developed a community engagement initiative, which involved a series of

Figure 4.1
The Point **Readership, 2013–2016**

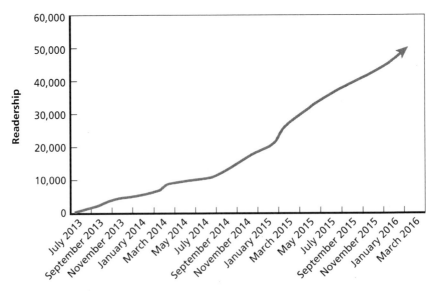

SOURCE: Multicultural NSW, 2016.

roundtable discussions between young people and various figures. This initiative included organising a dinner for a group of young people from predominantly Muslim backgrounds, who spoke with the United States Consul General in Sydney about their concerns about U.S. foreign policy in relation to Iraq and Afghanistan. One representative from Multicultural NSW noted that *The Point* is in many ways an extension of these roundtable conversations in that it provides space for authors, which may include young people, to air their views about controversial issues.

More directly, in an earlier community engagement project focused on facilitating discussion and opening up a safe space for youth to talk about contentious issues, staff from Multicultural NSW experimented with taking the discussions into social media by setting up a Facebook page. However, staff indicated that discussions "quickly degenerated" and "were not particularly productive in the online environment," noting that "while we could have those debates face to face and people would be passionate but still civil to each other, in the social media space, they tended not to be so civil."

As a result, Multicultural NSW launched *The Point* with the goal of creating an online space in which the organisation would intentionally address potentially contentious issues and situations directly. This approach would allow them to provide a forum for writers who may not otherwise expect to be given a government-funded and -sanctioned platform to express their views, and would allow discussion to be structured around more-thoughtful, longer-form written pieces than were likely to occur in simple back-and-forth exchanges through social media.

To a significant extent, the vehicle is also the message in the case of *The Point*. In the view of staff, *The Point* provides a space for "contentious and sensitive issues and [community members] know they are going to be given fair treatment by *The Point Magazine*." Of equal importance however, *The Point* is not just the "government consulting with the community and then the community never hears back from the government again," but instead in effect it is "the government saying . . . tell us what you think and we'll publish it next month."

The Point staff noted that, in the CVE community, when the online environment is considered, it is often viewed as a venue for promoting counter-narratives, and as a result, *The Point Magazine* is often thought of as being one. This, however, would be "an oversimplification—it is a community engagement tool."

The staff suggested that one potential approach that might inadvertently undermine CVE efforts—and conversely, a reason community engagement could be a powerful tool—was a failure to first address foundational issues. As one interviewee noted, "[There's] that talk in the CVE world about counter-narrative. . . . I think there's a lot of groundwork you need to do before you can simply present a counter-narrative to ISIS."

During interviews, *The Point* staff remarked several times on this notion of needing to do "groundwork" to build trust to enable the most important dialogues about more difficult issues to occur:

The starting point with a lot of our projects is that communities were just completely anti . . . anything CVE. And so that's the starting point where we had a lot of ground to make up.

The Point staff described an approach to community engagement that seemed to be focused on rebuilding trust within and between communities and government, with strong focuses on correcting misinformation in either direction (e.g., about a community, or about the actions of government or of extremists) and providing a space for community stakeholders, including those who might potentially be at risk of radicalisation themselves, to express their views openly in an organised way.

Critical to the process of building trust is addressing contentious issues head on and allowing potentially contrarian voices to be heard, all with the sponsorship of government support:

One of the ways you build trust in government is by correcting superstitions or conspiracies about government, explaining policies, allowing people a critical voice to come out and criticise various policies.

The Point staff saw correcting misinformation and communicating accurate information as critical components of their efforts. To this end, *The Point* staff described one of their strategies as "trying to educate the level of discussion going [on] within the communities, at the same time as giving them a voice." They also noted that, unaddressed, misinformation can cause damage and that "it reinforces government versus community kind of polarisation" and "distrust of government." *The Point*'s focus on the broader community is in part informed by a belief that misinformation at any level can have negative and cascading effects:

[A] lot of the work we do in CVE as a multicultural agency, including through *The Point Magazine* it is at that broader community level . . . people having conspiracy theories against government, but if we don't address that issue . . . then we're letting other problems fester and that can itself feed into some of the more pointy end problems in the CVE world.

The Point staff cited one example prior to the creation of the magazine, in which they funded a two-day educational workshop with Muslim community leaders at the University of Technology–Sydney addressing counterterrorism legislation. The workshop included presentations from officials involved in the task forces for Operation Pendennis and Operation Neath, two prominent Australian terrorism investigations. The sessions included a lawyer from the AFP, a representative from the Council for Civil Liberties, and a human rights lawyer. *The Point* staff cited two critical reasons for the success of the session. First, it was a balanced discussion around the issues and not simply the government presenting its information. Second, the case information that the government representatives presented were facts that were previously unknown to many in attendance:

> [Community leaders] turned around to me and said, "I had no idea that was what they were doing, I had no idea that's what the plot involved, I had no idea there was this evidence." . . . [T]his is coming from people who might've thought that CVE was just a made up issue, or there was a government conspiracy against the community, but if you actually give people the facts . . . they've never heard the facts before, they've never heard the policy rationale before.

Interviewees indicated that the stories *The Point* has chosen to address are

> issues that we knew the communities were talking about, or sometimes we knew that there was misinformation circulating around communities and social media networks, around a particular government policy or a misinformed argument about.

Because of its basis in community engagement, Multicultural NSW staff felt they had visibility into the issues and arguments circulating within communities and would write articles that "try to educate the level of discussion going on within the communities, at the same time as giving them a voice." Critical to restoring trust is giving community members a voice and treating issues in a fair and balanced way. The process and its results, as described by *The Point* staff, have been successful:

> We can go back to communities and they're willing to talk to us about these issues, because they can see that, A, we are listening to them, and, B, we are treating these issues in a balanced way. And then, C, we're also in the process actually trying to better inform the discussion within the communities as well around some of these issues.

While *The Point*'s primary visible activity consists of its online publication, staff described their efforts through the magazine as empowering communities to talk about violent extremism. This approach includes providing them with a space to talk, countering rumors and conspiracy theories about government, providing basic information to educate, and building up capacity within the community for those who may encounter radicalisation efforts targeted at themselves or may encounter individuals who have been targeted, and as a resource to communities. One interviewee succinctly summed up *The Point*'s approach in the following way:

> [O]ur whole philosophy has been that we need to facilitate a safe space where we can talk about these sensitive and contentious issues. And so our whole work has been about opening up that conversation in communities, not avoiding the topic and just talking about nice positive things in a social cohesion frame, and I think that's where our credibility has come from, not only with our government stakeholders and our funding bodies, but within the communities themselves. The communities themselves have actually started to recognise that actually what we're doing here is something quite edgy and interesting, and isn't it interesting that the government is actually allowing us to have this kind of conversation? . . . That actually allows then those voices within the community to come out and counter those more extreme voices within the community.

Evidence of Effectiveness

We did not have access to any evaluation material on the effectiveness of *The Point*. *The Point*, and CVE programs generally, would benefit from a full progress and impact evaluation.

Through the use of Google Analytics, Multicultural NSW is able to capture how many people, including how many unique users, have accessed *The Point*, how users access *The Point* (organic search, navigating directly to the site, or through a link posted on social media), what types of devices (desktop, mobile, or tablet) readers use to access the site, and what stories were most popular (Multicultural NSW, 2016).

Unfortunately, despite this, little is known about the magazine's true reach. Specifically, Multicultural NSW does not know where most readers are located, whether key target audiences (particularly youth or vulnerable communities) are accessing the magazine, how they feel about the content, and whether readers' attitudes are influenced by the site's material. As one of the interviewees from *The Point* team acknowledged:

> What we don't really know is what people are saying or commenting about *The Point* when they are sharing it. So we don't know whether they're saying they love it or they hate it, or, isn't this interesting, or, isn't it stupid.

This lack of in-depth knowledge about its audience means that it is difficult to determine how well *The Point* functions as a CVE initiative. The ongoing funding provided appears to have enabled Multicultural NSW to employ experienced journalists to develop and edit content for the magazine and invest considerable time in planning the magazine's content and maximising its exposure, resulting in a highly professional publication. Qualitative audience research is required to truly measure *The Point Magazine*'s impact and capacity to achieve its CVE and social cohesion goals. However, this type of research could reveal valuable insights into the demographic backgrounds of *The Point Magazine*'s readers, their purpose and motivation when accessing the magazine, and opinions about the articles they read.

CHAPTER FIVE

The Australian Multicultural Foundation: Community Awareness Training Manual— Building Resilience in the Community Program

Overview

AMF began delivering the Community Awareness Training Manual— Building Resilience in the Community program (CAT) in late 2013, and, as of late 2016, was continuing to deliver the program.[1] This program provides information to community members and service providers to assist them in recognising and countering the behaviours and processes that can lead to violent extremism. This training is delivered in two formats. First, it offers informational sessions for the general community or service providers. In parallel, it offers train-the-trainer sessions for community members and service providers who wish to subsequently conduct either of the program's two activ-

> **Facts About AMF's Program**
>
> **Group of focus:**
> - Individuals vulnerable to radicalisation
> - Friends and family
> - Communities
> - Social and healthcare workers
>
> **Unit of focus:**
> - Individual
>
> **Ideology:**
> - Religious
> - Political
> - Other
>
> **Intervention goal:**
> - Prevent
>
> **Activity type:**
> - Educational and mentoring
> - Informational
> - Enabling organisations

---

[1]   All interviews with program staff occurred on August 25, 2016.

ity types themselves (i.e., information sessions or train-the-trainer sessions) with other community members or providers.

In addition to offering materials on recognising behaviours, the training program and its accompanying manual also provide information to help communities cope with these behaviours and access other forms of support. The Australian federal government currently funds the initiative, but the program has also attracted Victorian state government funding for the program to be delivered across regional Victoria.

Goals and Approach to CVE

CAT staff members noted that, in their view, community participation is vital to counterterrorism and prevention, with there being a need for perhaps a "50/50" split between government-led counterterrorism efforts and community participation. Accordingly, an essential part of a CVE strategy is to determine how to engage the community itself to be a strong advocate for prevention.

CAT staff members say that, at its core, the program focuses on building resilience and preventing radicalisation that could lead to violent extremism. The primary means of achieving these goals is increasing awareness and understanding of the processes that can lead to radicalisation and of how to detect and recognise early warning signs and behaviours associated with radicalisation.

The program is designed to provide information to mothers, fathers, family and community members, and service providers about the processes by which individuals become radicalised—including alienation, unemployment, and other events and circumstances that may make individuals vulnerable to criminality or violence or spur already vulnerable persons to violence. It also focuses on training readers to recognise indicators and warning signs; works to dispel myths, misconceptions, and misinformation about radicalisation; and generally seeks to improve awareness and knowledge of prevention, including the importance of social cohesion and how to build community support networks and places communities can go for support.

However, while the program initially provided this information directly to youth, program staff found an appetite among various groups to be trained in how to provide the same information to others. Other community service providers, youth who had experienced radicalisation pressures themselves and wanted to help other youth, and other interested members of the community were interested in being trained to train others to provide the same information and assistance directly.

The program itself looks at a range of social processes that can lead a young person toward antisocial behaviour. Although one of these pathways is violent extremism, staff noted that the program was broader than this:

> It also acknowledges that ordinary Muslim families also have just as much issues regarding adolescent issues [as non-Muslim families do]—whether it's drugs or criminality or mixing with the wrong crowd, cultural differences, a whole range of things that may cause isolation, alienation, religious complexities, political complexities . . . domestic violence, all of those things.

Accordingly, program staff indicted that their curriculum looks at indicators that are relevant to a range of antisocial behaviours "that can lead to many different pathways," including but not limited to violent extremism. The scope and adaptability of the program, beyond being simply a CVE program, were, in the program staff's view, reasons for its success and why the community has embraced it. Indicators of radicalisation were, in this sense, only one of many things that parents needed to be educated on:

> What do an ordinary mum and dad know about radicalisation or extremism or terrorism. I mean, it's just like any other family, what would they know about recognising the early warning signs of domestic violence or drug abuse or whatever if you don't show them what the signs are?

Notably, CAT staff suggested that antisocial behaviours that were initially unrelated to violent extremism could inadvertently lead to radicalisation later, and thus it was critical to prevent those behaviours in the first place. One example cited by program staff was radicalisation within prisons: Youth could become involved in criminality for reasons that had nothing to do with violent extremism but, by starting down this path, were eventually arrested and then exposed to radicalisation pressures in prison they would not otherwise have encountered.

CAT staff said that underlying the design of the program is the Behavioural Indicators Model developed by Monash University (Australian Government, Attorney-General's Department, 2015, pp. 8–9). According to CAT staff, although the model has as many as 30 indicators, CAT uses only about 18 of them. In CAT's delivery, the indictors are used in conjunction with case studies, and participants are asked whether they agree that the indicators represent appropriate warning signs and whether they can suggest others.

The overall vision, in the words of one interviewee, is to help communities build capacity to resist radicalisation themselves:

[I]t is community based and it's meant to be adaptable and accessible so that communities can take the ownership and run it, because that's what, really, prevention's about in lots of ways, the capacities that they build and how they deal with it.

However, while the program is in many ways meant to be handed off to the community, CAT staff stressed that an important component was educating the community about the support systems that need to be built up around prevention efforts of this sort. Additionally, CAT staff remain active in setting up external support networks themselves, including access to scholars and religious leaders who could serve as resources. Furthermore, CAT staff reported that they contract as needed for matters beyond their in-house capabilities, including conflict resolution and psychological expertise. The program itself explicitly does not address mental health issues but provides access to support networks and can provide referrals.

Focus (Group of Focus, Unit of Focus, and Ideology)

The program targets a range of groups. CAT staff identified service providers as a key cohort, with a focus on those who provide youth services, but noted that they also go directly to young people themselves. Among service providers, the program works with community providers of youth services, police officers, and others who work with youth or communities. However, program staff noted that the program also currently "casually employs" a group of ten young people who have been trained to go out and train other young people and serve as peer mentors.

CAT staff noted that they felt they have been successful in identifying youth who are vulnerable to being, or in some cases have in the past been, radicalised and that they have had some success in reorienting these youth away from radicalisation. In turn, staff have found that these youth trainers are often well placed to identify people at risk of being radicalised and provide mentoring services, reaching groups and individuals that the AMF staff may not be able to on its own.

The CAT staff's method of recruiting participants for its sessions could be described as a "snowball" approach, working on referrals from participants and by word of mouth. CAT staff indicated that they believed if CAT advertised the sessions more broadly, its capacity would quickly be overwhelmed by the resulting demand.

Activity Type

The CAT training program is delivered in two primary formats: as a direct information session to the general community or to service providers, such as social workers and police community liaison officers, and as a "train-the-trainer" format for community members and service providers who wish to conduct informational sessions or provide the train-the-trainer program to others themselves.

At the time of the interviews with CAT staff, they had delivered 141 training sessions across Australia. Across those sessions, 425 participants had attended train-the-trainer sessions, and an additional

1,227 participants had attended the informational sessions. CAT staff indicated that they did not have data on how many additional informational sessions and train-the-trainer sessions may have been conducted outside the program by the 425 individuals it had trained to train others.

Generally speaking, informational sessions typically run about two and a half hours, while train-the-trainer sessions may run for a half-day. CAT staff's preparation time for the sessions varies based on the audience and the depth and intensity of training desired. Preparation for train-the-trainer sessions to hold informational sessions is generally more routine, while AMF has also engaged in more-tailored efforts for specific groups, such as city councils, which have requested more-customised curricula.

The information sessions target those who want to increase their knowledge and understanding and are designed for people such as parents, friends, peers, and mentors. Participants are given information about recognising early warning signs of radicalisation and how they can access assistance if they recognise warning signs in individuals from their communities. The AMF also does a "Welcome to Australia" course at many of its facilities across the country. AMF staff explained that the language, indicators, and case studies are translatable to other countries in Asia, the Middle East, and Europe. AMF has conducted informational sessions with officials from Indonesia, Thailand, Japan, the United Arab Emirates, and Qatar.

In contrast, train-the-trainer sessions are geared toward those who want to be able to train others, either formally or informally, and are very proactive, because participants must practice delivering the training they will eventually provide to others. The CAT interviewees suggested that these trainers may ultimately train others in a small group setting or work with others on an individual basis. The program has delivered training sessions throughout all states and territories in Australia. However, CAT interviewees suggested that most of their training sessions have focused on New South Wales, Victoria, and Queensland. Training sessions have also been delivered in Western Australia, Tasmania, South Australia, and the Australian Capital Territory.

In their training program, CAT staff use the Behavioural Indicators Model of radicalisation indicators from Monash University in Melbourne. Interviewees noted that a version of the Behavioural Indicators Model is also currently used by Australian law enforcement and counterterrorism agencies in their own programs. Furthermore, CAT staff noted that, in developing materials, they have been able to draw on input from families and individuals who have been directly affected by radicalisation themselves to ensure that materials resonate with and are consistent with the experiences of families who have had to confront these issues.

In addition to its primary training activities, CAT staff said that they had developed related materials, including a web application for mothers and families about how to create a safer social media environment for young children; an educational video using young Muslim actors who had volunteered to participate in going through scenarios, including a young person wishing to travel to Syria, an individual who had converted to Islam being confused about jihad, and a young woman being groomed on the internet for radicalisation; and an e-Learning platform for some of CAT's training.

The two CAT staff members responsible for delivering the training program have backgrounds in teaching and community development work. They both come from a strong teaching background but have 25 combined years of experience conducting training and leadership programs. The interviewees also said that their backgrounds in policy development and decades of community engagement work around a range of issues were invaluable in understanding of community needs, interests, and concerns and being able to communicate effectively with their target audiences. One interviewee stated that a background in community capacity-building and converting community consultations into "proactive programs" had proven valuable in developing CAT, which also involved considerable community consultation and input.

In addition, CAT staff reported that they provide support services for the young people they employ as trainers. As described by program staff, the support ranges from logistical support, to setting up workshops, to debriefings, to mentor groups, to psychological or professional support, if needed. However, staff stressed that a critical element of the program's success was the careful selection of the individual youth trainers themselves, many of whom are graduates of AMF leadership programs focused on public speaking, conflict resolution, and other core skills needed for their current duties.

Evidence of Effectiveness

The AMF evaluates its programs in a limited but formal and ongoing way. Each participant is asked to complete a post-training evaluation questionnaire consisting of three Likert scale questions and two open-ended questions designed to assess the relevance of and effectiveness of the training and manual.[2] In addition, the trainers themselves must complete a post-training questionnaire consisting of six open-ended questions designed to assess any challenges that the trainer encountered during the session, the ease of use of the Behavioural Indicators Model, and the participants' general response to the training.

The information gathered from these questionnaires not only is used internally to help identify opportunities for improvement, but also was also used by a third party in conjunction with information derived through telephone interviews to conduct a formal program evaluation as required by AGD.

The results of the evaluation indicated that both community members and service providers had positive views of the training. Both groups also agreed that the Behavioural Indicators Model is a useful tool in identifying behaviours and attitudes that signal a shift towards anti-social behaviours that could lead to violent extremism. Finally, the evaluation results suggested that the program has substantially increased the number of people equipped to deliver the training. These promising results, however, are more properly seen as elements of process or implementation—that is, they are measures of the extent

---

2   Likert scales allow users to express gradations of feeling in regard to the sentiment they are being asked about in a question (for example, whether they agree or disagree with a statement) rather than simply being able to answer yes or no.

to which the program was implemented and provided the services it intended to, not measures of whether those services achieved the intended objective. Ideally, the AMF should seek to evaluate whether key outcomes change as a result of the program: for example, whether participants were better equipped to detect and address radicalisation after the training than they were before the training. Similarly, while the program increased the numbers who could deliver a training, it did not assess how many did deliver that training, which would also be a useful performance measure.

CHAPTER SIX

Comparable CVE Programs in Europe and the United States

Introduction

The next phase of our work consisted of reviewing available information on CVE programs in Europe and the United States in an attempt to find programs that are comparable to *The Point* and to AMF's CAT. As previously noted, we focused on programs in Europe and in the United States and relied on open-source information. Generally speaking, information on CVE programs was more readily available for programs in Europe than for those in the United States, largely due to the availability of prior efforts in Europe to collect and consolidate information on CVE programs using a consistent format. In both cases, no single, truly comprehensive source of information was available.

Accordingly, it was beyond the scope of the study to characterize the extent to which there are programs in Europe or the United States that are truly similar to *The Point* and CAT. Similarly, we are unable to say how common programs with characteristics similar to *The Point* and CAT are. We simply focused on identifying a nonrepresentative set of programs with certain key characteristics similar to those of *The Point* and CAT and identifying some key similarities and potential differences between these projects and the two Australian programs. Within this group, we have also chosen to highlight programs that have conducted evaluations and have evidence of effectiveness or lessons learned.

Comparable European Programs

Using the methodology described in Chapter Two, we identified several CVE programs in Europe with similar characteristics to the two Australian programs.

Programs Similar to *The Point Magazine*

As discussed in Chapter Four, *The Point* is an online magazine, or, more broadly, an online set of resources, targeted at younger readers. Its goal is to inform its readers, engage them in a productive, positive dialogue, and provide a safe space to discuss controversial events, including overseas conflicts and the effect these conflicts have on local communities. *The Point* has a particular focus on social cohesion, and staff indicated that while *The Point* is characterised by some as a counter-narrative program, in their view it is also a community engagement tool. Many of *The Point*'s activities are focused on community engagement, but other activities provide an opportunity to vent opinions openly, and, in doing so, they provide an opportunity to engage in counter-narrative discussions. As will be discussed below, the European programs we found that were most similar to *The Point* tended to focus on providing counter-narratives. Accordingly, our comparison between *The Point* and these programs focuses on the counter-narrative aspects of the program, recognising that *The Point* is quite focused on expanding its reach into the community. Furthermore, although the European programs we found to be comparable tended to focus on counter-narratives, as previously noted this could simply be an artifact of the data that were available to us; there may be European programs that are similar to other aspects of *The Point*.

The importance of delivering alternative narratives to those presented by terrorist and extremist groups has long been recognised. In the European context, the first attempt at producing an orchestrated alternative narrative dates back to the 1970s, when, in the German Federal Republic, the government launched a national narrative challenging that of the terrorist group Red Army Faction (De Graaf, 2009). A wide array of programs focusing on alternative narratives mushroomed in Europe over the past decade, ranging from focused, in-person, one-to-one programs to broader, one-to-many, online campaigns. Below are a selection of approaches and practices developed in this field that most closely relate to the initiatives undertaken by *The Point*. Unlike *The Point*, however, the projects presented below generally take a more targeted approach to alternative narratives, focusing on directly deconstructing extremist propaganda or on providing their target groups with the instruments and knowledge required to defuse extremist rhetoric.

Cypher 7 A.D. and Abdullah-X[1]

The Cypher 7 A.D. (C7) program was created to provide online, creative content expressing the diverse ways in which Islam can be understood as a force for personal, societal, and political change. The idea behind C7 was that of helping young

> **Notable similarities:**
> - Online content
> - Addresses contentious or taboo issues
>
> **Notable differences:**
> - Strongly multi-media
> - Use of YouTube

people from Muslim communities use creative mediums to tackle and discuss issues ignored or considered taboo within their communities. On the now-defunct project website (Cypher 7 A.D., 2012), posters, videos, and comics were posted, touching on those issues and topics that youth may be afraid of discussing in their communities.

The C7 program led in 2012 to the establishment of the Abdullah-X project (Abdullah-X, 2015). Abdullah-X is a YouTube-hosted cartoon depicting a teenage Muslim boy who strives to understand his identity and role in society. The goal of this project is to challenge radical and extremist propaganda and narratives through an engaging and entertaining format. The cartoon's main character, Abdullah-X, is meant to represent an average young individual struggling with issues of identity, faith, belonging, sense of duty, and grievance.

Peer 2 Peer: Challenging Extremism[2]

Launched in June 2015, the Peer 2 Peer: Challenging Extremism (P2P) program is a global initiative that puts students from universities around

---

[1] The information in this section is from Radicalisation Awareness Network (2016) and European Commission (2014).

[2] The information in this section is from Radicalisation Awareness Network (2016).

the globe in a competition to produce innovative alternative-narrative campaigns and social media strategies against violent extremist propaganda (Peer 2 Peer: Challenging Extremism, undated). By stimulating different cohorts of students each academic semester into producing online or in-person strategies against extremism, the program develops credible campaigns that resonate with the communities and milieus students originate from. The program provides participating teams with a US$2,000 operational budget for designing, piloting, implementing, and evaluating their social or digital counter-extremism initiative. At the end of each semester, strategies implemented are assessed based on their results in accomplishing the following:

- motivating or empowering students to become involved in CVE
- catalysing other students to create their own initiatives, products, or tools to counter violent extremism
- building a community of interest or network focused on living shared values that also counter violent extremism.

The six best-performing initiatives are shortlisted for participation in further competitions, where two winners receive scholarship awards. The program is implemented by the EdVenture Partners consultancy, which assists students and their professors throughout the months of the program.

No-Nazi.net[3]

No-Nazi.net is an initiative launched by the Amadeu Antonio Foundation in Germany in 2011. The project is co-funded by the Amadeu Antonio Foundation and by the German Federal Ministry of Family Affairs, Senior Citizens, Women and Youth. The goal of this project is to build an online community of young people committed to combatting far right, racist, anti-Semitic, anti-Islamic, and hate propaganda. The project is online and encourages participants to monitor, evaluate, and combat propaganda on digital platforms by employing an alternative narrative underpinned by democratic values. The program targets

---

[3]   The information in this section is from Radicalisation Awareness Network (2016) and European Commission (2014).

youth in the 13–18 age group, providing them with peer coaching and training on how to counter extremist content online. Trained youth are then encouraged to take active roles in their social network spheres, combatting extremist propaganda. Similar training is also offered by the implementers to front-line educators.

In addition to these activities, individuals showing early signs of radicalisation are also approached by program implementers who chat with them to question their actions and provide them with an informative, critical analysis of the ideologies they are being lured by.

Evaluating Initiatives Presenting Alternative Narratives

Information was not readily available on the effectiveness of the three European programs similar to *The Point*, although all shared a common characteristic of presenting alternative narratives to counter radicalisation. Evaluating programs and initiatives presenting alternative narratives is considered challenging by practitioners and evaluators alike because of the inherent difficulty of measuring people's opinions and when and how they are changing. Although some of the projects presented above have reportedly been evaluated (Reynolds and Tuck, 2016), no publicly available evaluation reports could be identified by the time we completed this study.

Programs Similar to CAT

As discussed in Chapter Five, AMF's CAT provides information to community members and to service providers to assist them in recognising and countering behaviours that can lead to violent extremism. CAT delivers both informational sessions and train-the-trainer sessions for community members and service providers, while providing other support services. AMF staff described the program as at its core focused on building resilience and looking to prevent not only radicalisation but other dangerous behaviours that could put youth in jeopardy.

The development of a holistic approach to CVE in Europe has led to a growth in programs focusing on broader community engagement. Among these, a number of initiatives similar to CAT have been developed. These aim to empower key and vulnerable groups within communities to better understand and address phenomena such as violent extremism and radicalisation.

The ADFYWIAD Program[4]

The Advisory Directorate for Youth, Women and Imams' Active Development (ADFYWIAD) program was an initiative of the Muslim Council of Wales (MCW) aimed at preventing violent extremism and radicalisation. The program was sustained through funds from the Welsh Assembly Government (WAG) and from the broader

> **Notable similarities:**
> - Resilience building
> - Training
> - Radicalisation awareness
>
> **Notable differences:**
> - Broad/additional services
>
> *Evaluation available*

UK Government "Prevent" strategy.[5] The program ran between 2009 and 2012 and was implemented by the MCW and other nongovernmental organisations. The program focused both on local Muslim communities in general and on imams and the governance groups of mosques and other local Muslim organisations in particular. Similar to the CAT, the ADFYWIAD program aimed at building the resilience and ability of local communities to detect and tackle violent radicalisation through training. However, other capacity-building initiatives that were performed in the ADFYWIAD program have no equivalent in CAT. In particular, the ADFYWIAD also conducted the following activities:

- **Awareness raising program.** This activity aimed to increase awareness of the program and participation in its activities among target communities.
- **Governance and child protection training.** These training programs aimed at building the resilience of Muslim institutions and organisations and to ensure that they (1) operate in a context of good governance and child protection and (2) appreciate the importance of diverse representation in governance mechanisms.

---

[4] The information in this section is from Sheikh, Sarwar, and King (2012).

[5] *Prevent* is one of the four core elements of CONTEST, the UK Government's counterterrorism strategy. The *prevent* element aims to stop people from becoming terrorists or supporting terrorist organisations.

- **Engagement and training of all ADFYWIAD communities' audiences.** This program entailed the running of training programs aimed at developing the skills, awareness, and civic responsibility of target audiences, focusing particularly on (1) radicalisation and extremist ideology, (2) citizenship and civic responsibility, (3) partnership development between target audiences and statutory agencies (e.g., police), and (4) training sessions for Muslim leaders and community representatives to learn to identify and deconstruct extremist messages and transfer this knowledge to other community members.
- **iLead youth leadership project.** This developmental program focused on youth age 13 and older in an effort to increase their capability to act as leaders within their communities.
- **English language training and ijazahs for imams.** This program entailed classes aimed at improving the English language capabilities of imams, as well as the issuing of ijazah certificates to indicate which imams had been authorised to transmit religious knowledge.

An external evaluator performed process and outcome evaluation of the ADFYWIAD program in 2011. The evaluation employed a cross-sectional design, relying on a qualitative approach. The evaluation did not use a control group or quantitative methodologies, which could have helped strengthen the evidence presented. The evaluators first developed a theory of change model for the program on the basis of document review and stakeholder interviews. This theory was subsequently used as the evaluation framework of analysis for data collected through a small-scale online survey and stakeholder interviews.

The evaluation results suggest that there is evidence to support the claim that participants who joined the training were better positioned afterwards to support the Muslim communities they serve or are a part of. Participants interviewed highlighted the positive role that the training initiatives had in shedding light on important issues that had been overlooked until that point by local institutions. Interviewees also felt confident they would be better positioned to identify extremist arguments and to challenge them constructively. However, the evaluation found only limited evidence suggesting that the trainings and initiatives aimed at developing better partnerships and cooperation mechanisms among local Muslim institutions succeeded. Nonetheless, members of law enforcement agencies and local institutions indicated that the establishment of direct contacts and communication lines between them and Muslim communities had proven valuable and represented an important step towards closer day-to-day cooperation.

The evaluation identified several challenges and lessons learned. Both program implementers and evaluators highlighted the challenges they faced in recruiting mosques and Muslim community members to take part in their activities. In both instances, working in partnership with an organisation (i.e., MCW) with strong links and credentials with these communities proved fundamental for the success of the activities to be performed. Among the lessons learned, the evaluation highlights the positive effect made by the deployment of well-designed training sessions and experienced trainers. The evaluation also highlighted the importance of including interactive and practical sessions in the training programs so as to help participants cement their learning. With an eye to ensuring the sustainability of programs, evaluators also highlighted the positive impact that developing a class of new trainers—for example, using train-the-trainer methods during the sessions—could have for the project's future. Lastly, the evaluation highlighted the importance of ensuring that sufficient learning time is given to participants during training sessions to avoid overwhelming them with exceedingly large amounts of new concepts and information.

Young and Safe Project[6]

The Young and Safe project was established in 2009 in the London (UK) borough of Lambeth. Unlike the CAT training, the Young and Safe program focused on tackling serious youth violence connected to gangs, rather than on radicalisa-

> **Notable similarities:**
> - Avoiding unhealthy behaviours
>
> **Notable differences:**
> - Gang-focused
> - Broad, additional services
>
> *Evaluation available*

---

6 Much of the information in this section is from Krafchik and Ryszkowska (2011).

tion and violent extremism (Vidino and Brandon, 2012). In particular, the Young and Safe program worked with young people age 8–19 identified as involved or at risk of involvement with criminal activity, gangs, and violence. Nonetheless, the preventative and disengagement initiatives run as part of this program provide lessons that could be transferred to programs focusing on violent radicalisation and extremism, such as CAT.

The interventions implemented by the program operated both at the individual and group levels and aimed at avoiding participants' future involvement, or facilitating the withdrawal of those engaged, in violent activities. A range of group-based interventions were implemented as part of the program:

1. **You-Turn.** This initiative aimed at changing the attitudes and behaviours of young men through a focus on health and other well-being issues.
2. **2XL.** This initiative consisted of weekly sessions focusing on themes of identity, culture, goal-setting, peer pressure, and law. Participants attending were also encouraged to pursue career opportunities made available through the program.
3. **Fix-Up.** This intervention targeted 14–19-year-olds and consisted of weekly awareness-raising sessions on gangs and crime, employing audio-visual presentations interspersed with activities and discussion.
4. **Young People Matter/group mentoring.** This initiative run by grassroots organisations entailed a range of different activities, including career development programs for 16–19-year-olds, workshops and lunch-time activities for secondary schools, and one-to-one mentoring for pupils.
5. **K-Artz.** This initiative targeted kids from top years of primary school and entailed weekly sessions of arts-based activities and visits to a go-karting centre. This intervention encouraged children to make friends with those from other schools and groups, to break up the tribal nature of social interaction within the borough.

The Young and Safe project also featured a range of one-to-one interventions, for example:

1. **Into Adulthood.** A full-time program of academic tuition, physical exercise, and personal, social, and career development.
2. **Career Development Program.** A series of individual sessions focusing on planning for the future and accompanied by group sessions.
3. **Safer Choices.** An initiative targeting young women, providing them with weekly meetings focusing on considering what constitutes a healthy relationship.
4. **Exclusion.** An intervention providing four hours of personal tuition and ten hours of mentoring support to young people excluded from school, engaging them in sport and leisure activities in an attempt to establish normal routines in their lives.

An external evaluator performed a process and outcome evaluation of the Young and Safe program between 2010 and 2011 (Krafchik and Ryszkowska, 2011). The evaluation employed a cross-sectional design, qualitative interviews, and observations. No medium- to long-term follow-ups are presented in the evaluation, thus limiting the assessment of the influence and results achieved by the program in these time frames.

The evaluation found that the Young and Safe program appeared to be fulfilling a crucial role with young people in the Lambeth borough, particularly through interventions targeting the 13–17 age group. This age group was identified as one where participants could still be positively influenced and levered away from violent and criminal lifestyles. More broadly, evaluators found that, for both group and individual interventions with different age groups, evidence indicated that participants were reflecting on and rethinking their attitudes and aspirations.

The evaluation highlighted several lessons learned from the program implementation. First, evaluators highlighted the importance that group-structured interventions played. Participants stressed that group dynamics and the creation of a cohesive cohort through meetings were key factors facilitating participants' retention across weeks. Interviewees stressed that special bonds and relationships had been created and that these could prove a valuable source of support and resilience beyond the end of the program. Participants' engagements were also reportedly facilitated by the fact that the interventions were not run by governmental authorities but were rather seen as distinct from these. One issue interviewees lamented was the lack of safe places to return to and of activities to engage in outside of regular school hours. With regard to the evaluation, the evaluators raised concerns about the small sample size of interviews conducted, which limited their ability to draw general conclusions about the overarching program.

Comparable U.S. Programs

Because a coordinated, national focus on CVE efforts in the United States began only recently—especially when compared with Europe and Australia—identifying comparable U.S. programs was difficult. We were not unable to identify a U.S. program similar to *The Point* using the methodology described in Chapter Two, but we were able to identify a program similar to CAT. The lack of findings regarding U.S. programs similar to *The Point* should not be regarded as indicating that they do not exist, but simply that we were unable to identify one within the relatively limited scope of the study.

Programs Similar to CAT
The World Organization for Resource Development and Education

The World Organization for Resource Development and Education (WORDE) is a "non-profit, educational organization whose mission is to enhance communication and understanding between diverse communities to mitigate social and political conflict" (WORDE, 2016). WORDE's CVE efforts

> **Notable similarities:**
> - Radicalisation awareness
>
> **Notable differences:**
> - Model-based
>
> *Evaluation available*

focused on creating and maintaining the very networks of civically engaged individuals, who are sensitized to issues of violent extremism, and who have proactive, cooperative relationships with local social services and law enforcement agencies. (Williams, Horgan, and Evans, 2016)

WORDE uses a "portfolio" approach to its CVE programming, meaning that rather than employ a single program, it uses a combination of community education, action programs, and collaboration building between law enforcement and community partners (Williams, Horgan, and Evans, 2016). This portfolio is called the Montgomery County Model (MCM).[7]

The MCM's core objective is to generate public awareness about the potential risk factors of violent extremism and to empower the appropriate figures to intervene with vulnerable individuals before they choose a path of violence. The four components of the model are engaging partners, educating stakeholders, connecting the public to vital resources, and intervening when necessary (WORDE, 2016). This initiative is executed through the Faith Community Working Group, an official body within the Montgomery County Executive's Office of Community Partnerships, which works with both WORDE and nongovernmental community stakeholders to develop a specific programming agenda (WORDE, 2016). This programming agenda consists of a variety of activities and events including a number of training and information sessions delivered to different groups. From 2013 to 2016, this program has engaged more than 4,274 county residents (WORDE, 2016).

A comprehensive evaluation of the program's effectiveness was conducted from 2014 to 2016 by outside researchers under the auspices of the U.S. Department of Justice. This evaluation of a U.S. community-based CVE program was intended to provide evidence-based insights into the effectiveness of the MCM, as well as measurement instruments and common metrics that could be used to evaluate other CVE programs (Williams, Horgan, and Evans, 2016). Using

---

[7] In 2016, the MCM was renamed as the Building Resilience Against Violent Extremism (BRAVE) model to give it more general applicability.

data collected from program participants through surveys and focus groups, the results of the study suggested that the program was successful in creating "intended effects on 12–14 outcomes believed to be CVE-relevant."[8]

Using the results of this study combined with the experience, lessons learned, and best practices garnered from managing the program, WORDE created a comprehensive training curriculum designed to "guide communities, including law enforcement and local government agencies, with building positive and collaborative relationships with diverse Muslim communities, understanding the potential risk factors of radicalization and mobilization to violent extremism, and creating a community-led engagement model to counter violent extremism" (Mirahmadi and Farooq, 2016). Titled *Developing a Community-Led Approach to Countering Violent Extremism (CVE): An Instructor's Manual*, the curriculum is designed as an interactive, multimedia course divided into three modules, which can each be taught as stand-alone lessons that provide other organisations a step-by-step roadmap to implementing a successful CVE strategy using the MCM. The manual includes teaching notes, facilitator notes, student handouts, lesson objectives, discussion questions, engagement tips, quizzes, lesson summaries, group activities, and additional reading lists. In addition, the manual is designed to offer the flexibility to tailor the lessons to meet the specific needs of a particular audience. WORDE recently released a 2016–2019 strategic plan, which aims to "institutionalize what WORDE started to develop organically in Montgomery County, Maryland, document good practices, and establish WORDE's strategy for replicating the program across the National Capital Region [Washington, DC metropolitan area] and beyond" (WORDE, 2016).

---

[8]   Williams, Horgan, and Evans, 2016. This study focused on participants of WORDE's volunteer-service and multicultural programming but did not include an evaluation of the training curriculum.

CHAPTER SEVEN

Findings and Conclusions

Findings

In total, our review identified three European programs with characteristics similar to *The Point*, two European programs with characteristics similar to CAT, and one U.S. program with characteristics similar to CAT. As noted earlier, we regarded programs as having similar characteristics if they had generally similar goals and activity types to either program. Three of the six programs we identified had available evaluation material that might be of use to program staff in Australia; while we did not identify this information for the other three programs during the course of the study, it may also be available and simply was not identified during the study period.

The programs we identified are not necessarily a representative sample of CVE programs in Europe and the United States with goals and activities similar to those of *The Point* and CAT. Similarly, our characterisation of key program similarities and differences was based on a review of only open-source information and may miss, or mislabel, key aspects of these programs.

Nevertheless, in addition to identifying a set of programs with similar goals and activities that may benefit from sharing information between their respective staffs and those of *The Point* and CAT, some interesting characteristics did begin to emerge. First, programs identified as counterparts to *The Point* appeared to have strong online presences and communities. Areas where they differed from *The Point*, and that may interest *The Point* staff, were engagement methods for their target groups—ranging from the award competition run by Peer2Peer to the empowerment efforts of NoNazi.net—and the use of wider varieties of media, including cartoons, YouTube, and other formats in Cypher 7 A.D. and Abdullah-X.

Second, the European programs seemed to take more-direct approaches to developing alternative narratives than *The Point* did. Whereas *The Point* seemed to take a more subtle approach of allowing a safe space for conversation, allowing government-funded expression of support for opinions of all types, including those counter to the government (as long as not violent), the European programs more directly engaged in developing alternative narratives, either asking young people themselves to do so or providing target groups with information to defuse extremist rhetoric. Whether either approach is superior and, if so, in what context are important questions for future research that were beyond the scope of this study.

Unsurprisingly, all of the alternative narrative programs targeting young people, including *The Point* itself, employed the internet, a home website, social media, and digital communications. Given *The Point's* earlier and somewhat trying experience with social media, it appears likely that the respective programs could benefit from sharing lessons learned and strategies regarding this approach. In this, and in all cases, it is not only that the Australian CVE programs may benefit from lessons learned from the programs in Europe and the United States but that the European and U.S. programs may benefit from lessons from the Australian experience.

The three programs similar to CAT seemed to share a common trait in that they provided fairly broad bases of services. This is not necessarily dissimilar from CAT, because interviews with CAT staff suggested that the program provided a host of other services when needed, which may have changed over the years of program operation based on demand. However, the services offered by the European and U.S. programs may have been more explicit and ongoing distinct program components than their counterparts in CAT. Regardless, the more notable finding may be the suggestion that programs of this nature appear to commonly offer a suite of services and activities to participants, rather than providing a single service in isolation. Whether this approach is effective, what the ideal mix of services might be, and in what context are important questions for future research.

Conclusions

While individual programs may offer promising results, an effective CVE effort is likely to require an entire system of programs, operated across a range governmental and nongovernmental organisations, and targeting diverse aspects of radicalisation, ranging from direct interventions with at-risk individuals to community-level programs. These programs should probably be designed both to raise awareness and to build productive relationships with national and local-level institutions and authorities.[1] Unfortunately, to the extent that CVE efforts have been studied, the majority of evaluation efforts to date have focused on assessing individual programs, rather than on developing a comprehensive systems approach to evaluate broader CVE outcomes. Australia—and any other nation—is likely to require a system of complementary and coordinated efforts to counter violent extremism effectively. Lacking such a framework, efforts to prevent or address violent extremism may be or become disjointed, lack coordination across government and nongovernmental agencies, and ultimately fail to meet desired objectives. The characteristics identified by IMPACT Europe and used in this study—group of focus, unit of focus, ideology, intervention goal, and activity type—provide one such framework that could be used to provide a standardised means of describing and characterising CVE programs. Using a shared set of commonly identified and important characteristics to begin to develop a taxonomy of program types is a natural first step toward more robust evaluation not only of individual programs but of systems for CVE.

Accordingly, several additional research efforts may be needed. First, CVE efforts should likely be assessed using a systems approach.

---

[1]   Consider the notion of vertical or "linking" capital, which is about forming relationships between individuals and communities with institutional and formal power structures in a society. See Szreter and Woolcock (2004).

Even in the small community of programs included in this study, it was clear that the programs often served multiple groups, with a variety of services. It was also clear that programs of one general "type" (for example, providing a safe place for youth to discuss contentious issues) may benefit from coordination with other program "types" (for example, programs to train and empower family and community members to recognise signs of radicalisation). Notably, while this study included government-funded efforts, it did not address inherently government-designed and -implemented operations, such as law enforcement, and the key roles these agencies play in CVE. Key remaining research questions in this area include the following:

- What components—for example, government agencies, nongovernmental entities, and community and stakeholder partners—need to come together for a comprehensive CVE effort?
- What do these components need to do—what programs, activities, coordination, and collaboration—to effectively fight HVE?

The first phase of such an effort should simply be descriptive and should attempt to answer the question: What types of *programs* currently exist, how are they structured, and what services and activities are they undertaking? A second phase would be evaluative and would attempt to answer a second question: What programs *should* exist, how should they be structured, and what services and activities should they undertake, based on evidence?

One way to address these questions may be to visualise CVE efforts as comprising three levels: strategic, operational, and tactical. In this framework, the **strategic level** refers to the national approach to CVE, including the national vision, funding, strategy, and plan for CVE. Analysis at this level would consist of reviewing national-level strategic guidance, funding levels, and policy. The **operational level** would describe the types of programs that are being undertaken to implement the strategic vision, concentrating on the focus area and mix of program types, including the balance between programs focused on prevention, mitigation, deterrence, detection, or enforcement. The **tactical level** refers to specific program models to identify which models are most effective for achieving their respective program goals. This analysis should be conducted not only within Australia, the United States, and the many nations of Europe but also across these so as to identify promising models and lessons learned at each level.

Our study was able to focus only on the tactical level of CVE, by conducting a limited comparative analysis of a small number of programs. Critically, while we looked at only a small number of programs, we were also not able to assess the respective contexts of the programs that were included. Efforts of this nature should be greatly expanded to answer key questions at the tactical level:

- How should CVE programs be characterised and classified? What are the key characteristics of a CVE program? Are there a small number of common types of CVE programs?
- What CVE programs currently exist, by type?
- Which existing CVE programs are similar to one another? In what ways are they similar and different?
- What specific programs and program models and types work? Why do they work, and in what contexts?

Such work should be undertaken as soon as possible. The need for effective CVE efforts is unfortunately all too self-evident. However, even the limited review of programs conducted for this study suggests that there are a large number of ongoing CVE efforts underway, which may provide a significant opportunity to share knowledge and improve effectiveness.

Illustrative Overview of Australian CVE Programs

Table A.1 lists some of the CVE programs that have been funded by the Australian government since roughly 2010. Some were funded by the LST program and others by the Building Community Resilience/ Youth Mentoring Programs, which was a pilot and cancelled in 2012. We understand from discussions with HA that the CVE/LST website is being updated, but also that many of the programs funded through CVE grants are sensitive and as such are not publicly available. Still, we believe that this illustrative list shows the variety of CVE programs funded by the Australian government over time and is worthwhile to include, even if incomplete and slightly out of date.

Table A.1
Illustrative Overview of Australian CVE Programs

Program	Location	Provider	Category	Description
Australian Muslim Youth Leadership and Mentorship Program	Nation-wide	The Australian Multicultural Foundation	Youth Mentoring	Sixteen young Australian Muslim leaders from around Australia will be given the skills and resources to represent their communities. The purpose of this project is to engage with the broader community to dispel myths and misconceptions about Islam. Following intensive training, these youth leaders will complete specific tasks including peer mentoring and consulting with communities to inform the development of a national youth-led event for Muslim and non-Muslim youth.
Teaching Democracy—political extremism, global lessons for local educators	Australian Capital Territory	The Federation of Ethnic Communities' Councils of Australia	Building Community Resilience	The project will deliver a two-day workshop for school teachers to explore the theoretical concepts and practical implications behind extreme political action, including radicalism and extremism. The workshop will provide training and information for teachers to influence a positive development of young people's political consciousness and encourage their constructive participation in society. The Federation of Ethnic Communities' Councils of Australia will use the outcomes of the workshop to develop teaching support resources that could be distributed widely to schools.
Aussie Youth Connect	NSW	Anglicare Sydney	Youth Mentoring	This project will train and develop young people to become peer mentors to other vulnerable and disadvantaged youth. The project includes an eight-week training program on topics such as leadership, alternatives to violence, and social resilience. Mentors will build community relationships and create opportunities for engagement with young people who have exhibited anti-social behaviour or are at risk of being extremist or resorting to violence.

Table A.1—continued

Program	Location	Provider	Category	Description
Building resilience to violent extremism in the Canterbury-Bankstown region: a focus on our youth	NSW	The Youth Centre	Building Community Resilience	The project will focus on youth in the Canterbury-Bankstown region aged between 13 and 25 who have been exposed to some form of violent extremism, are at risk of being exposed to extremist messages, or may be sympathetic to or already influenced by extremist messages and ideologies in the community. It will develop programs that challenge extremist messages and ideologies, including those perpetuated online, and provide avenues for the non-violent expression of views and encourage participation in our democratic society.
Different People Different Voices Project (DPDVP)	NSW	Burwood Council	Building Community Resilience	DPDVP is a youth (12–24yrs) community project aimed at building resilience to cultural isolation and increasing community belonging, through the production of a regional youth service map supported by an intercultural interactive board game (generating the "experience" of living in a setting of cultural cohesion and no cultural tolerance and the impacts). The project focuses on peer-to-peer development, community engagement, and leadership to create awareness of risk factors that may lead to violent extremism and develop localised protective factors at an early stage for young people experiencing disengagement and marginalisation.
Dream Big Project	NSW	Auburn Community Development Network Inc.	Building Community Resilience	The proposed project is a mentoring and skills development program that will give young people the real-life experience of creating, operating, and managing a shared business venture. Participants will be mentored to develop skills and confidence in the various aspects of business, such as marketing and sales, finance, human resources, management, product design and development, research and development, and administration. Working in a team environment, participants will also have the opportunity to explore the various cultures and religious and non-religious beliefs and practices that exist in the diverse communities that make up the area.

Table A.1—continued

Program	Location	Provider	Category	Description
Football United–Fairfield Liverpool Youth Exchange	NSW	School of Public Health and Community Medicine, University of New South Wales	Building Community Resilience	The project will deliver weekly football coaching programs and Gala Days for younger children representative of their community. Regular football offers youth the chance to build camaraderie and learn from peer mentors in a safe, active environment. As coaching sessions are the primary activity for the Football United program, participants get to connect, exchange, and learn on-field fair play values that are intended to be replicated in life off the field. The participants are required to attend, engage, and behave in school in order to be eligible to partake in the program. The project will work to establish effective resilience and leadership building workshops, set up group mentoring programs (by Football United community coaches), and provide media and social networking education to project participants.
Mentoring and Resiliency Development Project	NSW	JobQuest	Youth Mentoring	This project is designed to facilitate effective social interaction among vulnerable young people in culturally diverse environments. Through group training and individual mentoring, the project will assist participants to deal with conflicts and handle frustrations encountered in daily life. Families and community members will also be involved in the program to help model acceptable behaviours and improve the psychosocial well-being of the participants.
Sharing Humanity	NSW	The Lebanese Moslem Association	Building Community Resilience	The project will seek to develop young Muslim leaders (10 males and 10 females) through developing their skills and confidence to influence members of their peer group and the community at large. The project will work to build understanding and equip Muslims with the theological fundamentals that counter extremist ideologies, dispel misconceptions and develop their role as citizens, leaders, and positive role models so that they can become "leaders" for mainstream Islam and assert their Australian identity.

Table A.1—continued

Program	Location	Provider	Category	Description
Somali Community Resilience Project	NSW	Australian Somali Community Association	Building Community Resilience	The Somali Community Resilience Project will address the growing level of disengagement by young people in the Somali community by strengthening their resilience to radicalisation. The project will develop support and cultural community programs such as forums, mentoring programs, and a conference to empower young people in the Somali community to connect and engage with their local community. At the conclusion of the project, the Australian Somali Community Association along with other project partners will develop an ongoing and sustainable community development program, using the Australian Somali Community Association's volunteer resources
Somali Youth Outreach Project	NSW	Horn of Africa Relief and Development Agency of Australia Inc.	Building Community Resilience	The project will develop forums/workshops for at-risk Somali and other at-risk youth groups between the ages of 16 and 24. The workshops will support the program participants to identify difficulties and issues their peers are facing and encourage their peers to seek the appropriate help to deal with these issues. They will also increase understanding among young Somalis and other youth groups of the negative impacts of extremist views and actions on individuals and broader society. Participants will also be encouraged to attend a leadership youth camp in Melbourne at which they can share experiences with other young people in contributing positively and becoming responsible citizens in the wider community.

Table A.1—continued

Program	Location	Provider	Category	Description
Southern Crescent On-line Peace Initiative	NSW	Forum on Australia's Islamic Relations Inc.	Building Community Resilience	The project will create an interactive website/portal geared for youth. The portal will include live chat sessions and commonly asked questions answered by international Islamic scholars to promote and educate youth about the positive and moderate calling of Islam and expand on various meanings and interpretations. As part of the project, a short video documentary (15 minutes) will explore intercultural or interfaith issues and will focus on three themes: initiating peace, building cohesion, and working towards action. This will be a youth-led project supported by experienced filmmakers as mentors.
Empowering Youth to Say No to Radicalisation	Queensland	Islamic Council of Queensland	Building Community Resilience	The project will aim to develop counter-narrative messages to challenge Islamic militancy propaganda through the use of guest speakers and workshops involving academics, Queensland Police, and imams. With established networks within congregations, these entities will encourage youth who have a fear and mistrust of authority to participate positively in the Australian way of life, encompassing the values of freedom, fair play, mateship, and tolerance.
Aman: Youth for Peace-Building	Victoria	Australian Muslim Women's Centre for Human Rights	Youth Mentoring	Aman is a peace-building project that promotes mentoring programs among young people through school-based activities including group discussions, assignments, and creative team projects. An Islamic secondary schools' conference will also be run as part of the project, giving teachers the opportunity to reflect on the challenges and barriers that Muslim youth experience and develop mentoring skills and strategies to address these issues.

Table A.1—continued

Program	Location	Provider	Category	Description
Audio/Film Production for Youth Engagement and Training	Victoria	Islamic Council of Victoria	Building Community Resilience	The Audio and Film Production program will provide an opportunity for Muslim youth to engage in learning how to use sound design, sound editing, and audio mixing to create soundtracks and movies. This project is designed to assist disadvantaged Muslim youth to develop effective techniques, including assistance in crafting positive messages that will have long lasting effects. The project will encourage young people to participate in development projects that will support them in expressing their views creatively and positively.
Building Community Capacity in Nonviolent Leadership: An interfaith program for Young People	Victoria	Pace e Bene Australia Inc.	Building Community Resilience	Pace e Bene Australia will design and deliver a national interfaith/intercultural youth development program in Melbourne to skill future leaders to provide alternatives to violence in their communities through inclusion and tolerance. The project will focus on collaboration with a variety of universities, theological colleges, multi-faith networks, and cultural groups to invite 20 young leaders showing potential for active leadership in their communities to engage in an eight-day program with two residential retreats in early 2012.
CONNECT @ The Huddle	Victoria	The North Melbourne Football Club	Building Community Resilience	CONNECT @ The Huddle will target 15–25-year-olds to connect young people with learning, recreation, employment opportunities, technology, community, and each other. The project will support young people in developing their own arguments and messages to challenge and contest extremist ideologies through ongoing dialogue. Community leaders, role models, peers, academics, and elite professional sports people will be involved in elaborating and delivering messages through the CONNECT program to enhance individual identity and a sense of community belonging, reduce social isolation, and create resilient leaders among young people to be better equipped to contest extremist messages and violent radicalism.

Table A.1—continued

Program	Location	Provider	Category	Description
Curbing Radicalisation through Youth Resilience and Community Partnerships	Victoria	Victorian Arabic Social Services	Building Community Resilience	The project will develop and facilitate a series of workshops and activities aimed at building resilience by providing avenues for positive expression and mutual understanding of diversity. Activities for Arabic-speaking youth living in the municipalities of Hume, Moreland, and Hobson's Bay will engage young people by providing them with opportunities to express themselves (such as through making a computer game, creating a short film, media training, and utilising media outlets, such as youth radio and television).
Development of a common curriculum Framework in Islamic Studies for Islamic Schools (NCEIS)	Victoria	The University of Melbourne	Building Community Resilience	In collaboration with the leadership and teachers of selected Islamic schools and Muslim peak bodies, the NCEIS will design and develop a Common Curriculum Framework (CFF) for teaching Islamic Studies in Australian Islamic primary and secondary schools. The CCF will help to create discerning students, who are able to differentiate mainstream, traditional Islam from violent extremism. Subjects, such as the Qur'an and Islamic History, will be presented with adherence to traditional principles. Acknowledging Australia's multicultural context, the CCF will also include a range of new topics that address issues relevant to Muslims in Australia, such as Islam and the modern state, Islam and women, and Islam and other faiths.
Hume Anti-Violent Extremism Youth (HAVEY) Project	Victoria	Hume City Council	Youth Mentoring	This project will foster mentoring networks and cross-cultural understanding between young people from different ethnic groups. Mentoring activities will focus on issues such as the needs of young people within their families and communities, improving their decisionmaking skills, and providing prevention or early intervention support. Mentees will also design and participate in community celebrations.

Table A.1—continued

Program	Location	Provider	Category	Description
iAct Interfaith Youth Leadership Program	Victoria	InterAction Multifaith Youth Network Inc.	Building Community Resilience	The "iAct" interfaith youth leadership program will bring together young people from diverse faith backgrounds to build bridges of understanding and cooperation to break down stereotypes and work together on community-service projects. Through this process, the participants explore their own religious identities, learn about others, and gain knowledge and skills to contribute positively to their communities.
inSite Projects	Victoria	Youth Development Australia Ltd.	Youth Mentoring	This project will bring together four groups of eight to ten young people from marginalised and disadvantaged culturally and linguistically diverse backgrounds to collaborate in producing multimedia works centred on the ideas of tolerance, understanding, community, and cultural sharing. Through the semester-long project, young people will be mentored by multimedia practitioners, who will facilitate intensive workshops, giving the young people skills they need to create their multimedia pieces. In the final stages of the project, participants will be offered training in presentation skills and will be made available to schools and community groups to talk about their involvement and present their documentaries.
Media Makers	Victoria	Multicultural Media Exchange	Youth Mentoring	Media Makers is a media training and mentoring program to link young Muslim Australians with professional journalists to produce news stories that reflect the concerns, interests, and character of multicultural Australia. The project training and activities will foster citizenship, encourage a culture of rational dialogue and debate, and give participants the tools and avenues to communicate effectively both within their communities and across the broader Australian public.

Table A.1—continued

Program	Location	Provider	Category	Description
More Than a Game	Victoria	Footscray Football Club Ltd	Building Community Resilience	Spirit West Services will work together with young men (15 to 25 years) to support people who may be vulnerable to extremist views due to personal experiences of disengagement and marginalisation. The project will use sport to engage with the young men to address issues of harmony, cultural identity, and social cohesion to provide an avenue for the non-violent expression of views and encourage participation in the local community. Through group training and individual mentoring, the project will focus on empowering young people to improve their decisionmaking capabilities and equip them with skills and resources to understand and actively address intolerant or extremist messages.
Salam Alaykum "Darebin's Muslims Reaching Out"	Victoria	City of Darebin	Building Community Resilience	The program will build community connections and engagement between Darebin's Muslim community and the broader Darebin community. It will also build the Omar bin Al-Kattab Mosque's capacity to manage community relations to develop and implement strategies that prevent the development of risky extremist views that can threaten community cohesion. The project will involve youth from the Muslim community to run team building activities with a focus on encouraging them to be more trusting of one another and encourage a positive connection with the wider community.
Unite 4 Justice	Victoria	Centre for Multicultural Youth	Youth Mentoring	The Unite 4 Justice program aims to support young people from diverse cultural backgrounds in developing practical strategies for promoting the values of shared freedoms, tolerance, and a commitment to democratic values and principles. The project will work with 30 young people from five or six secondary schools and their communities to develop leadership skills, facilitate dialogue, and, with the support of mentors, deliver five or six youth-led projects that promote respect and build community resilience.

Table A.1—continued

Program	Location	Provider	Category	Description
Voices of Change	Victoria	Spectrum Migrant Resource Centre	Youth Mentoring	Voices of Change will empower youth ambassadors aged 18 to 28 and provide them with skills to be mentors for other young people. The project will include mentoring training and discussion sessions that explore community issues that could contribute to intolerant or extremist views. An inter-faith camp will also be run to bring together young people from various communities and faiths to debate issues around extremism.
Young Muslim Leadership Development: A Program in Social Dialogue and Community Resilience	Victoria	La Trobe University	Building Community Resilience	The project will develop a training program, resources, and a network for young people to help create an environment in which young Australian Muslims are aided and empowered to play socially constructive leadership roles in their respective communities. The structure of the project also provides an opportunity for these leaders to gain greater prominence among Muslim intellectuals in the wider Australian and international communities.
Beyond Bali Education Kit	Western Australia	Bali Peace Park Association Incorporated	Building Community Resilience	The project will develop an education resource for secondary school students (years 8 and 9) on the Bali bombings and the Bali Peace Park. The resource is designed to build social resilience to violent extremism by discussing issues like the social impact of violent extremism and encouraging students to think about how societies can resist the influence of violent extremism.

SOURCE: Australian Government, 2018a.

U.S. DHS-Funded CVE Programs

Table B.1 provides an overview of the programs awarded funding through DHS's OCR Grants program.[1]

---

[1] Program details were not available for some of the 31 grant recipients.

Table B.1
U.S. DHS-Funded CVE Programs

Program	Location	Provider	Category	Description
The Takeoff	Minneapolis, MN	Ka-Joog	Developing Resilience	This program is a free educational after-school program for youth who typically lack access to the necessary resources and services needed to help them succeed academically, socially, mentally, and physically.
Be@School	Minneapolis, MN	Ka-Joog	Developing Resilience	This program is designed to increase school attendance and improve community connections across Hennepin County through a collaborative early intervention providing education and support services to school-age youth and their families.
Fanka (The Arts)	Minneapolis, MN	Ka-Joog	Developing Resilience	This program creates an intimate space for the community in Minnesota to motivate, empower, and elevate each other through the arts, including poetry, music, theatre, storytelling, painting, sculptures, and more.
Empowering U	Minneapolis, MN	Heartland Democracy Center	Developing Resilience	This program is a deep empowerment and civic engagement program that uses discussions, readings, values, activities, and stories to engage participants in meaningful ways and to provide some basic civics education and skills for participants to operate and thrive in their communities and the wider world.
Common Bond	Nationwide	Tuesday's Children	Developing Resilience	This program brings together young adults, age 15–20, from around the world who share a "common bond"—the loss of a family member due to an act of terrorism, violent extremism, or war.
Christian-Muslim Peacemaking	Nationwide	Peace Catalyst International Inc.	Developing Resilience	"Christian-Muslim Peacemaking 101" is an online course on the basics of becoming a "peacemaker." There is also a "Peacemaking 201," the follow-on course, which also provides opportunities for hands-on experience and pairs those taking the course with mentors.

Table B.1—continued

Program	Location	Provider	Category	Description
Houston CVE Training and Engagement Initiative	Houston, TX	City of Houston, Mayor's Office of Public Safety & Homeland Security	Training and Engagement	The Houston Countering Violent Extremism (CVE) Training and Engagement Initiative will be led by a Houston Regional CVE Steering Committee to produce scenario-based workshops for parents and youth, as well as a train-the-trainer program to ensure sustainability of the initiative. It will include a modular and flexible approach to training, workshops, and information sharing that is adaptable to a wide range of venues and mechanisms of delivery.
Targeted Violence Prevention Program (TVPP)	Illinois	Illinois Criminal Justice Information Authority	Training and Engagement	TVPP uses a public health approach towards ideologically inspired targeted violence prevention. TVPP works with interested communities in building and sustaining community-level programs that can prevent individuals from being recruited to commit ideologically inspired targeted violence, and to help redirect or "off-ramp" individuals who have not yet committed a crime. The program leverages existing resources that can benefit individuals and organisations.
Cross Community Engagement (CCE) Program	New Jersey	Global Peace Foundation	Training and Engagement	CCE engages at-risk youth from five ethnic groups: Latino, African American, Asian Indian, Caucasian, and Arabs. Over a 12-month period, these youth will participate in a series of workshops, field trips, and activities designed to build cross-cultural relationships. Through this pilot initiative, the Global Peace Foundation intends to demonstrate a national model for replication and to measure the empirical impact on identity-based attitudes and behaviours.

Table B.1—continued

Program	Location	Provider	Category	Description
No program name given	Nebraska	Nebraska Emergency Management Agency	Training and Engagement	Grant money will be used to identify barriers that keep peers or family members from reporting potential signs of radicalisation using a public-health approach. The CVE project will be used in rural or small to mid-sized city public health departments. In addition to identifying barriers to reporting, the program will develop strategies to address them. Other goals include increasing awareness of observable behaviours associated with the process of radicalisation and enhancing the connection between state-level threat assessment resources and local trusted resources receiving reports.
No program name given	Denver, CO	Denver Police Department (DPD)	Training and Engagement	Utilising a multi-pronged approach, DPD will focus on officer training, school-based mentoring, and refugee/immigrant outreach.
ExitUSA	Nationwide	Life After Hate Inc.	Managing Interventions	Using former members of the American violent far-right extremist movement, this program helps radicalised individuals disengage from extremist movements and begin the process of de-radicalisation. The program also supports community practitioners (counselors, social workers, faith leaders, etc.) and families who are working with individuals who have the desire to change.
Safe Spaces	Nationwide	Muslim Public Affairs Council Federation	Managing Interventions	Safe Spaces is an alternative to both heavy-handed law enforcement tactics and government-led CVE programs. Rather than accepting the notion that the only way to deal with terrorism is through tactics such as widespread surveillance and the use of informants, Safe Spaces relies on community-led and community-driven programs that communities and mosques will benefit from beyond the national security context.

Table B.1—continued

Program	Location	Provider	Category	Description
United Against Violence	Reno, NV	Project Help Nevada, Inc.	Challenging the Narrative	Project Help Nevada will partner with KOLO News, University of Nevada–Reno, and the Bosma group to implement a CVE media campaign. The primary objective of the United Against Violence coalition is to target the average community member to help change the status quo through a positive, prosocial counter-narrative.
My Fellow American	Nationwide	Unity Productions Foundation	Challenging the Narrative	This program is an online film and social media project that calls upon concerned Americans to spread a message that Muslims are our fellow Americans. It asks people of other backgrounds to share a real-life story about a Muslim friend, neighbor, or colleague that they admire. Using the power of social media, My Fellow American seeks to change the narrative from Muslims as the other to Muslims as fellow Americans.
It's Time: ExOut Extremism	Nationwide	Rochester Institute of Technology (RIT)	Challenging the Narrative	It's Time: ExOut Extremism is a social media campaign aimed at countering terrorist propaganda online. With the grant funding, RIT will expand its campaign to include a new online platform that uses targeted campaigns to reach at-risk individuals and communities, to support speaking tours and trainings to a network of mosques and Muslim organisations, and to aid efforts to catalog, record, and distribute Muslim American stories.
No program name given	Nationwide	University of North Carolina at Chapel Hill	Challenging the Narrative	Grant money will fund a project to create a series of sophisticated videos and other materials to counteract jihadist propaganda that targets young people. The videos will be produced by Carolina students—experts in understanding how to communicate with their peers, what video games and movies are popular, what messages will feel authentic—in conjunction with university faculty who are experts in jihadist propaganda, video and gaming production, and persuasion strategies.

Table B.1—continued

Program	Location	Provider	Category	Description
Digital Disruption	New York, NY	Counter Extremism Project (CEP)	Building Capacity	Digital Disruption seeks to identify, expose, and report the profiles and accounts of extremists on Twitter, Facebook, YouTube, Ask.fm, and other social media networks. CEP monitors profiles in multiple languages, including English, Arabic, French, Italian, German, and Turkish.
Promoting Equality and Civic Engagement	Los Angeles, CA	Claremont School of Theology	Building Capacity	This project aims to generate positive outcomes by providing scholarly perspectives, professional expertise, and organisational best practices to organisations seeking the resources and support to excel in pursuit of their goals. The program will provide a training series and sub-grants to applicant organisations to develop new programs that meet the needs of their respective communities in terms of religious literacy, civic engagement, cultural competency, social justice advocacy, and related areas.

SOURCE: DHS, undated-b.

Survey Instrument

Part I: Survey Instrument: Basic Program Identification

Program name	
Website	
Contact information for the person(s) most responsible for currently managing the program	Name: Title: Address: Phone: Email: Name: Title: Address: Phone: Email:
City in which program operates	(If multiple cities, list all; if another type of community, describe)
Program length (years/ months)	How long has your program been in existence?
Motivation for program	Can you tell me a bit about the origins of [Program Name]? Why was [Program Name] started?

Program materials (Any shared written materials such as reports, data, or other materials)	Sample Question: Do you have any program materials, like brochures, worksheets, advertisements, that we could see? • No • Yes If yes, describe materials and name of file on SharePoint where materials are stored:

Part II: Survey Instrument: Program Type/Theories of Change

Major focus Overarching goal(s)	Programs like yours have different focuses or goals. How would you describe your program's goals? [IF NEEDED Would you say the focus is....] • Prevention • Deradicalisation • Other (Please specify)
Intervention, Services or activities	Can you tell me about all of the activities or services you provide as part of [program name]? (Ask for detailed description of each activity) Subsequent questions include: • What is the goal of the activity or intervention? • How might this activity or intervention work to counter or address extremism? • How long are participants exposed to the treatment? // How often do people participate in the program activities? • Approximately how many people have received/ been exposed to the intervention?

Specific Focus (Examples include: address alienation, correct religious ideology, promote positive community, heal mental health problems, crisis intervention, improve sympathy with victims)	What is the goal of the activity or intervention?
Theory of change	How might this activity or intervention work to counter or address extremism?
Intervention length (Examples:) If film screening, likely 2 hours If therapy, perhaps 8 week course If community center open through high school, perhaps 34 years	SELECT MOST APPROPRIATE QUESTION: How long are participants exposed to the program? Number of contacts e.g., number of times the person receives services: How often do people participate in the program activities? Unit of time sessions, hours, days, weeks, months, as needed, no specified time limit (or 'other,' describe):
Inclusion	Who does the activity or intervention try to serve or reach?

Participants served	How many people is the program serving? Does the number fluctuate?

Part III: Survey Instrument: Outreach Strategies

Program communication	Sample Question: How do people find out about the program? IF NEEDED: Do people generally come to [Program Name] after hearing about it through... • Flyers • Posters • Mailings • Internet • Word of mouth • Community referrals (schools, other community organisations, specify) • Other (specify)
Activities to increase participation (Examples include longer hours, more service sites, changing a name to be less stigmatising, etc.)	Sample Question: What type of changes or adaptations to the program have you needed to make to help increase participation in [Program Name]?

Part IV: Survey Instrument: Evaluation

Self Assessment Identify types of documentation that are kept on the participants served; obtain as much detail as possible. This should include information on any measurement they do related to participants, including things like customer satisfaction surveys, repeated administrations of instruments, etc.	The goal of our interviews is to develop a toolkit to help programs evaluate their programs' effectiveness. To do this, you need data. What type of data do you collect, if any, on your program to help you gauge how effective it is and how you could improve it? OUTCOME DATA: PROCESS DATA: (Examples: Treatment exposures, Films produced, Messages disseminated, Workshops completed, etc) [IF THEY COLLECT DATA]: How is the data stored?

Assessment approaches	IF COLLECTING DATA//ASSESSING IMPACT: How are you currently measuring your programs success or evaluating its own efforts?
Program changes	IF COLLECTING DATA//ASSESSING IMPACT: What types of changes or adaptations to the program have you made/do you plan to make based on your evaluation?
Self-Assessment	IF NOT COLLECTING DATA//ASSESSING IMPACT: If you are not currently measuring your program's success, I understand. Can you tell me why not? What do you think is the biggest challenge to assessing program impact?
Future planned changes	What type of changes or adaptations to the program are you planning and why have you decided to make these changes?

Part V: Other Programs

Other related programs	Do you know of any other programs that you think we should speak with for our research project?
	Name of Organisation: Contact Person: Contact Email: Contact Phone: Name of Organisation: Contact Person: Contact Email: Contact Phone: Name of Organisation: Contact Person: Contact Email: Contact Phone: Name of Organisation: Contact Person: Contact Email: Contact Phone: Name of Organisation: Contact Person: Contact Email: Contact Phone:

Part VI: Follow-up

Follow-up	Would it be ok if we called you back to clarify any of the information you provided to us today? • Yes • No
	We would like to send a summary of the program information to you to verify. Can I confirm that the contact information I have for you is correct?

Remind interviewee about any documents that they have agreed to share; coordinate practicalities!	

Part VII: Administrative Information

Date	Date of conversation:
RAND staff	Lead Interviewer: Note taker:

References

Abbott, Tony, and George Brandis, "Counter-Terrorism Measures for a Safer Australia," joint press release, August 26, 2014. http://parlinfo.aph.gov.au/parlInfo/search/display/display.w3p;query=Id%3A%22m edia%2Fpressrel%2F3357815%22

Abdullah-X, homepage, 2015. As of November 21, 2018: http://www.abdullahx.com/

AMF—*See* Australian Multicultural Foundation.

Australian Government, *Counter-Terrorism White Paper: Securing Australia, Protecting Our Community*, 2010. As of January 15, 2019: https://www.dst.defence.gov.au/sites/default/files/basic_pages/documents/counter-terrorism-white-paper.pdf

Australian Government, "Living Safe Together: Get Involved," webpage, 2018a. As of November 20, 2018: https://web.archive.org/web/20180313073642/https://www.livingsafetogether.gov. au/getinvolved/pages/home.aspx

Australian Government, "Living Safe Together: Partners: Government," 2018b. As of November 20, 2018: https://web.archive.org/web/20180313081115/https://www.livingsafetogether.gov. au/partners/Pages/government.aspx

Australian Government, "Living Safer Together: Partners: Researcher Community," webpage, 2018c. As of November 20, 2018: https://web.archive.org/web/20180313081139/https://www.livingsafetogether.gov. au/partners/Pages/research-community.aspx

Australian Government, Attorney-General's Department, *Preventing Violent Extremism and Radicalisation in Australia*, 2015. As of November 20, 2018: https://web.archive.org/web/20180313072507/https://www.livingsafetogether. gov.au/informationadvice/Documents/preventing-violent-extremism-and-radicalisation-in-australia.pdf

Australian Government, Department of Home Affairs, "Welcome to the Department of Home Affairs," webpage, accessed 2017. As of November 20, 2018: https://www.homeaffairs.gov.au/

Australian Multicultural Foundation, "Community Awareness Training Manual—Building Resilience in the Community," website, undated. As of November 20, 2018: http://www.amf.net.au/entry/ community-awareness-training-manual-building-resilience-in-the-community

Australian National Audit Office, *The Design of, and Award of Funding Under, the Living Safe Together Grants Programme*, September 1, 2016. As of November 20, 2018: https://www.anao.gov.au/work/performance-audit/ design-and-award-funding-under-living-safe-together-grants-programme

Brandis, George, "Opening Statement, International Meeting on Counter-Terrorism," August 10, 2016a. As of November 21, 2018: https://web.archive.org/web/20170228011112/https://www.attorneygeneral.gov.au/ Speeches/Pages/2016/ThirdQuarter/Opening-statement-International-Meeting-on-Counter-Terrorism.aspx

Brandis, George, "Keynote Address, CDPP'S Annual Counter-Terrorism Conference, Sydney," September 20, 2016b. As of November 21, 2016: https://web.archive.org/web/20170228011038/https://www.attorneygeneral.gov. au/Speeches/Pages/2016/ThirdQuarter/Keynote-address-CDPPS-annual-counter-terrorism-conference-sydney.aspx

Brandis, George, and Michael Keenan, "Attorney-General's Portfolio Budget Measures 2016–17," joint media statement, May 3, 2016. As of November 29, 2018: https://www.ag.gov.au/Publications/Budgets/Budget2016-17/Pages/Media-Releases/Attorney-Generals-Portfolio-Budget-measures-2016-17.aspx

Council of Australian Governments, *Australia's Counter-Terrorism Strategy: Strengthening Our Resilience*, 2015.

Cypher 7 A.D., homepage, 2012. Archived at: https://web.archive.org/web/20161021063255/http://www.cypher7ad.com

De Graaf, Beatrice, "Counter-Narratives and the Unrehearsed Stories Counter-Terrorists Unwittingly Produce," *Perspective on Terrorism*, Vol. 3, No. 2, 2009.

DHS—*See* U.S. Department of Homeland Security.

European Commission, *Preventing Radicalisation to Terrorism and Violent Extremism: Strengthening the EU's Response*, 2014. As of November 20, 2018: http://www.europarl.europa.eu/meetdocs/2009_2014/documents/com/ com_com(2013)0941_/com_com(2013)0941_en.pdf

European Commission, *The European Agenda on Security*, COM(2015) 185 Final, April 28, 2015. As of November 20, 2018:
https://eur-lex.europa.eu/legal-content/EN/TXT/?qid=1485257048405&uri=CEL EX:52015DC0185

European Commission, "European Union Steps Up Efforts to Prevent Violent Extremism and Counter-Terrorism in the Middle East and North Africa," press release, September 14, 2017. As of November 20, 2018:
http://europa.eu/rapid/press-release_IP-17-3225_en.htm

Grossman, M., M. Peucker, D. Smith, and H. Dellal, *Stocktake Research Project: A Systematic Literature and Selected Program Review on Social Cohesion, Community Resilience and Violent Extremism 2011–2015*, Melbourne: Community Resilience Unit, Department of Premier and Cabinet, State of Victoria, 2016. As of November 20, 2018:
http://www.amf.net.au/library/uploads/files/15412_Stocktake_Research_Program_V13_(1).pdf

Harman, Hakan, Kavita Bedford, and Widyan Fares, "About," *The Point Magazine*, webpage, 2018. As of November 20, 2018:
http://www.thepointmagazine.com.au/about.php

Harris-Hogan, Shandon, Kate Barrelle, and Andrew Zammit, "What Is Countering Violent Extremism? Exploring CVE Policy and Practice in Australia," *Behavioural Sciences of Terrorism and Political Aggression*, Vol. 8, No. 1, 2015.

Helsel, Phil, "Australia Christmas Terror Plot Foiled, Police Say," NBC News, December 22, 2016. As of November 20, 2018:
https://www.nbcnews.com/storyline/isis-terror/australia-christmas-terror-plot-foiled-police-say-n699381

IMPACT Europe, *Innovative Method and Procedure to Assess Counter-Violent-Radicalisation Techniques in Europe*, 2015. As of November 20, 2018:
http://impacteurope.eu/wp-content/uploads/2015/02/D2.2-Synthesis-Report.pdf

Institute for Economics and Peace, *Global Terrorism Index*, 2015. As of November 20, 2018:
http://economicsandpeace.org/wp-content/uploads/2015/11/Global-Terrorism-Index-2015.pdf

International Association of Chiefs of Police, Committee on Terrorism, Countering Violent Extremism Working Group, *A Common Lexicon*, 2012. As of November 20, 2018:
http://www.theiacp.org/portals/0/pdfs/IACP-OT_CommonLexicon_Eng_FINALAug12.pdf

Khan, Humera, "Why Countering Extremism Fails," *Foreign Affairs*, February 18, 2015.

Krafchik, M., and Y. Ryszkowska, *Evaluation of Young and Safe Project: London Borough of Lambeth*, Dudley, UK: Inspira Consulting, 2011.

McCelland, Robert, "Budget 2010: Countering Violent Extremism in Our Community," media release, Parliament of Australia, May 11, 2010. As of November 20, 2018:
http://parlinfo.aph.gov.au/parlInfo/search/display/display.w3p;query=Id%3A%22m edia%2Fpressrel%2FL4PW6%22

Mirahmadi, Hedeieh, and Mehreen Farooq, eds., *Developing a Community-Led Approach to Countering Violent Extremism (CVE): An Instructor's Manual*, World Organization for Resource Development and Education, 2016.

Multicultural NSW, *The Point Magazine: Program Report*, Australia–New Zealand Counter-Terrorism Committee, May 2016, not available to the general public.

Peer 2 Peer: Challenging Extremism, homepage, undated. As of November 21, 2018:
http://edventurepartners.com/peer2peer/

Radicalisation Awareness Network, *Preventing Radicalisation to Terrorism and Violent Extremism: Approaches and Practices*, 2016.

Reynolds, Louis, and Henry Tuck, *The Counter-Narrative Monitoring and Evaluation Handbook*, London: The Institute for Strategic Dialogue, 2016.

Romaniuk, Peter, *Does CVE Work? Lessons Learned from the Global Effort to Counter Violent Extremism*, Goshen, Ind.: Global Center on Cooperative Security, September 2015. As of November 20, 2018:
http://www.globalcenter.org/wp-content/uploads/2015/09/Does-CVE-Work_2015.pdf

Sheikh, Sanah, Shama Sarwar, and Ewan King, *Evaluation of the Muslim Council of Wales' Prevent Work*, Welsh Government Social Research, 2012. As of November 20, 2018:
https://gov.wales/docs/caecd/research/120719muslimcouncilen.pdf

Szreter, S., and M. Woolcock, "Health by Association? Social Capital, Social Theory and the Political Economy of Public Health," *International Journal of Epidemiology*, Vol. 33, No. 4, 2004, pp. 650–667.

The Point Magazine, "Edgy Multiculturalism for a New Generation," November 2017. As of November 20, 2018:
http://www.thepointmagazine.com.au/post.php?s=2017-11-29-edgy-multiculturalism-for-a-new-generation

The Point Magazine, homepage, 2018. As of November 21, 2018:
https://thepointmag.com/

United Nations Security Council, Resolution 2178, September 24, 2014.

U.S. Department of Homeland Security, "Countering Violent Extremism Task Force," webpage, undated-a. As of November 20, 2018:
https://www.dhs.gov/cve

U.S. Department of Homeland Security, "DHS Countering Violent Extremism Grants," webpage, undated-b. As of November 20, 2018:
https://www.dhs.gov/cvegrants

U.S. Department of Homeland Security, *Empowering Local Partners to Prevent Violent Extremism in the United States*, Washington, D.C., August 2011a.

U.S. Department of Homeland Security, *Strategic Implementation Plan for Empowering Local Partners to Prevent Violent Extremism in the United States*, Washington, D.C., October 2011b.

U.S. Department of Homeland Security, *Strategic Implementation Plan for Empowering Local Partners to Prevent Violent Extremism in the United States*, Washington, D.C., October 2016.

U.S. Department of Homeland Security, "Statement by Secretary Jeh Johnson Announcing First Round of DHS's Countering Violent Extremism Grants," press release, January 13, 2017.

U.S. Department of Justice, *Fact Sheet: UN Security Council Resolution 2178 on Foreign Terrorist Fighters*, undated. As of November 20, 2018:
https://www.justice.gov/file/344501/download

U.S. Department of Justice, Office of Community Oriented Policing Services, *Homegrown Violent Extremism: Awareness Brief,* Washington, D.C., 2014. As of November 20, 2018:
https://web.archive.org/web/20171023025216/http://www.theiacp.org/Portals/0/documents/HomegrownViolentExtremismAwarenessBrief.pdf

Vidino, Lorenzo, and James Brandon, *Countering Radicalisation in Europe*, International Centre for the Study of Radicalisation and Political Violence (ICSR), 2012.

Williams, Michael, John Horgan, and William Evans, *Evaluation of a Multi-Faceted, U.S. Community-Based, Muslim-Led CVE Program*, Washington, D.C.: U.S. Department of Homeland Security, 2016.

WORDE—*See* World Organization for Resource Development and Education.

World Organization for Resource Development and Education, *The Building Resilience Against Violent Extremism (BRAVE) Model: Strategic Plan, 2016–2019*, 2016.

About the Authors

Andrew Lauland is a senior policy researcher at the RAND Corporation and former director of homeland security and homeland security advisor for the state of Maryland. Lauland has an M.P.P. in public policy, administration, and analysis, and his research focuses on law enforcement and criminal justice.

Jennifer D. P. Moroney is a senior political scientist at RAND and served as the inaugural director of RAND Australia. Moroney has a Ph.D. in international relations, and she specializes primarily in European and Eurasian politics, security cooperation strategy and evaluation, and operational analyses and lessons.

John G. Rivers is a Coast Guard officer who served as a Federal Executive Fellow at RAND from 2016 to 2017. As of 2019, he is assigned to the Pentagon as Coast Guard Liaison to the Chairman of the Joint Chiefs of Staff.

Jacopo Bellasio is an analyst at RAND Europe, where he focuses on defence and security issues. Bellasio has an M.Litt. in Middle East and Central Asian security studies.

Kate Cameron is a senior analyst at RAND Australia whose research has focused technology futures and forecasting and national security. Cameron has a Ph.D. in mathematics and served as the first Australian Defence Science and Technology Group Liaison Officer within the Special Operations Research and Development Center (SORDAC) in U.S. Special Operations Command.